People of the Spirit:
The Story of God and His People
STUDENT GUIDE: Study One

J. Ben Wiles

OVERVIEW

In this first volume of *People of the Spirit: The Story of God and His People*, Christians find their place in the grand story of redemption. This seven-week journey of story and Scripture spans the entire Bible from Genesis to Revelation, with guided discussions for small group study and thoughtful questions for individual reflection. People of the Spirit aims to work with the Holy Spirit to transform and empower the reader, not just convey information.

All Scripture quotations, unless otherwise indicated, are taken from The Holy Bible, *New International Version* ®, NIV ® Copyright © 1973, 1978, 1984, 2011 by Biblica, Inc. ® Used by permission. All rights reserved worldwide.

Scripture quotations marked NKJV are taken from the New King James Version. Copyright © 1982 by Thomas Nelson, Inc. Used by permission. All rights reserved.

ISBN: 978-1-940682-37-2

Copyright © 2015 by Church of God Adult Discipleship

All rights reserved. No part of this publication may be reproduced, stored in a retrieval system, or transmitted in any form or by any means—electronic, mechanical, photocopy, recording, or any other—except for brief quotations in printed reviews, without the prior permission of Church of God Adult Discipleship.

Printed in the United States of America.

Table of Contents

GROUP COVENANT 5

WEEK 1 9

    DAY 1—FORBIDDEN FRUIT.. 9

    DAY 2—HIDING FROM GOD 17

    DAY 3—KNOWLEDGE AND BLAME 21

    DAY 4—EDEN LOST 25

    DAY 5—A GLIMMER OF HOPE.................................31

WEEK 2 35

    DAY 1—THE CALL OF ABRAHAM 35

    DAY 2—EXODUS FROM EGYPT 45

    DAY 3—A HOLY PEOPLE...51

    DAY 4—THE PROBLEM WITH IDOLS.......................55

    DAY 5—AN IMPORTANT DECISION 61

WEEK 3 67

    DAY 1—NO OTHER GODS 67

    DAY 2—REMEMBER THE SABBATH.........................75

    DAY 3—RIGHT RELATIONSHIPS 81

    DAY 4—REVERENT FEAR...85

    DAY 5—THAT PROPHET 89

WEEK 4 93

    DAY 1—DAVID'S THRONE..93

DAY 2—A NEW START 101

DAY 3—SMALL THINGS 107

DAY 4—A NEW HEART 111

DAY 5—COMFORT MY PEOPLE 117

WEEK 5 121

DAY 1—A NEW DAY DAWNS 121

DAY 2—JESUS' BAPTISM AND TEMPTATION 129

DAY 3—JESUS' DEATH 135

DAY 4—JESUS' RESURRECTION 141

DAY 5—JESUS' ASCENSION 147

WEEK 6 153

DAY 1—ASCENSION AND COMMISSION 153

DAY 2—PENTECOST 161

DAY 3—PERSECUTION AND EXPANSION 167

DAY 4—ONE NEW HUMANITY 171

DAY 5—EDEN RESTORED 177

BIBLIOGRAPHY 185

Group Covenant

Instead, speaking the truth in love, we will grow to become in every respect the mature body of him who is the head, that is, Christ. From him the whole body, joined and held together by every supporting ligament, grows and builds itself up in love, as each part does its work (Ephesians 4:15-16).

It is hoped that each individual undertaking the *People of the Spirit* process will experience transformation and growth in Christlikeness over the course of the experience. But individual growth alone is not enough. It must take place in the context of relationship with others of the same faith, each one building the others up so that all become mature followers of Jesus Christ and, as a result, fully functioning participants in God's plan to save creation.

With that in mind, before continuing with the study, each member of the group should agree to the following covenant with one another. Please read and reflect upon the following statements and indicate your commitment to the group by signing your name at the bottom. Then each member of the *People of the Spirit* group should sign one another's group covenant so that everyone's copy has every signature of the group. Keep this group covenant in your book for future reference as needed.

PRIORITY: The group meeting will be a priority in my schedule. If I am running late or unable to attend, I will contact my group leader.

PREPAREDNESS: I realize that what I put into the lesson is what I will get out of it. Therefore, I will prepare for the lesson each week and come prepared to share.

RESPECT: Everyone has a right to their opinion and all questions are encouraged and respected. I will listen attentively to others without interrupting them.

CONFIDENTIALITY: Anything of a personal nature that is said in the meeting should not be repeated outside the meeting. This group is intended to be a safe place for open discussion and sharing.

HONESTY: I will strive to be real, honest, and transparent with the other group members.

SUPPORT: The mission and values of the group have my support and I will refrain from gossip or criticism.

SIGNATURES

DATE

Week 1

Day 1

Forbidden Fruit

Learning the Story

In the beginning was God. God is love. God's love was so powerful it overflowed, and so He began to create. Each time He created something He said, "It is good." God is good, so everything God created is good. That includes us.

He made the first man, Adam, out of the dust of the earth and breathed the breath of life into him. Then, so Adam would not be alone, God created the first woman, Eve, out of Adam's side. He placed Adam and Eve into the Garden of Eden and they were to walk together in God's presence and tend the garden. They were told to be fruitful and multiply, to fill the earth, and to expand the borders of

10 WEEK 1

Eden. They had all of God's creation at their fingertips as resources to fulfill their purpose. They perfectly reflected the glory of God. They had God-given dominion over the things on earth as they walked in unbroken fellowship with Him. But there was one tree from which they were forbidden to eat, and that tree is where the problem begins.

In Genesis 3, the serpent tempted Eve to eat the fruit and she did. She then gave it to Adam to eat, and he did as well. In that moment, the relationship between God and humans became corrupted. Where once Adam and Eve reflected the glory of God in the earth, now that image had been distorted. In this act of disobedience, they made the choice to live by their own rules instead of by their dependence on God's Spirit.

Because of their willful disobedience, Adam and Eve had to leave the garden. What once had been easy now became difficult. They would have to coax food out of the ground by the sweat of their brow. Childbirth would become traumatic. Within one generation, the first murder would take place. Generation after generation, humanity would look and act less like their Creator with dire consequences, including the flood that almost wiped out

DAY 1: FORBIDDEN FRUIT 11

humanity. A curse had fallen on the same creation that at one time God had said was good. God knew this was going to happen, so He set in motion a plan to save all of His creation, including humanity.

Searching the Scripture

Read Genesis 3:1-6:

> Now the serpent was more crafty than any of the wild animals the Lord God had made. He said to the woman, "Did God really say, 'You must not eat from any tree in the Garden'?"
>
> The woman said to the serpent, "We may eat fruit from the trees in the Garden, but God did say, 'You must not eat fruit from the tree that is in the middle of the Garden, and you must not touch it, or you will die.'"
>
> "You will not certainly die," the serpent said to the woman. "For God knows that when you eat from it your eyes will be opened, and you will be like God, knowing good and evil."
>
> When the woman saw that the fruit of the tree was good for food and pleasing to the eye, and also desirable for gaining wisdom, she took some and ate it. She also gave some to her husband, who was with her, and he ate it.[1]

---

[1] All Scripture, unless otherwise indicated, is taken from the *New International Version*, 2011.

12 WEEK 1

Answer the following questions:

- What was the first question in the serpent's conversation with Eve?

- Compare Genesis 2:15-17 with Genesis 3:3. How are they the same? How are they different?

- What argument did the serpent use to finally convince Eve to eat the fruit?

- How did Eve justify eating the fruit?

- What was Eve's first act immediately after she ate the fruit?

DAY 1: FORBIDDEN FRUIT 13

Yielding to the Spirit

Know

- When Adam and Eve chose to eat the forbidden fruit, they chose to usurp God's authority over them. In other words, they discovered a different way to live—a life where they wouldn't need God to tell them what was right and what was wrong. They would do that for themselves. Where have you seen this tendency to choose our way over God's way in the world around us? How is it affecting humanity culturally, relationally, and economically?

14 | WEEK 1

- In what ways have you seen the evil one try to distort God's instructions in your life? Have you ever chosen your own way instead of doing things God's way? What happened when you did?

Be

- Ask the Holy Spirit to show you where you have made your desires more important than God's will for your life. Be honest with Him as He reveals these areas to you, so that He can work with you to change your heart and align your desires with God's will for your life. Use the space below to write what He is saying to you.

DAY 1: FORBIDDEN FRUIT 15

Do

- Take your list to the Lord in prayer. Begin by repenting for insisting on your own way over His will. Acknowledge that His will is good, and that you know He loves you and wants to bless you. If you have not already done so, this is an excellent time for you to decide to surrender your life to follow Him. If you would like to do that, talk with your discipleship partner or group leader right away and they will walk you through the steps to begin your new life in God!

Remember, as part of the journey of becoming people of the Spirit, you must reach out to those around you in prayer and evangelism. Renew your commitment today to the following two things:

- I will participate with my church family through my prayer, regular attendance, financial support, and ministry involvement. Specifically, I want to serve in the area of _____.

16 WEEK 1

- I will reach out to those who are not yet following Jesus by regularly praying for the following people to be saved:

Day 2

Hiding From God

Searching the Scripture

Read Genesis 3:7-9:

> Then the eyes of both of them were opened, and they realized they were naked; so they sewed fig leaves together and made coverings for themselves. Then the man and his wife heard the sound of the Lord God as he was walking in the Garden in the cool of the day, and they hid from the Lord God among the trees of the Garden. But the Lord God called to the man, "Where are you?"

Answer the following questions:

- What was the first sign that something had changed after Adam and Eve had eaten the forbidden fruit?

18 WEEK 1

- What was the first couple's solution to the issue of their nakedness?

- What was their response when they heard the sound of God walking in the garden?

- What was the question that God called out to Adam? Why do you think God asked this question in this way? Was it because He didn't know the answer or was there possibly another reason?

DAY 2: HIDING FROM GOD   19

Yielding to the Spirit

Know

One of the first things we do when there is sin in our lives is attempt to hide it. We try to take matters into our own hands by covering up our mistakes out of shame. Another tendency we have when there is sin in our lives is to hide from God. This is often reflected in our reluctance to worship, to pray, or to even be around God's people.

Be

Ask the Holy Spirit to reveal places in your life where you are attempting to cover for your mistakes or hide from God in some way. Be open to areas that the Spirit may speak to you about that you haven't been aware of before.

What feelings do you get about God when you think about Him, or when others are talking about Him? Do you feel fear, rejection, or anger? Do you feel His love for you? Allow the Holy Spirit to show you the love of God that was best demonstrated in the giving of His Son, Jesus, to make

20 **WEEK 1**

forgiveness and hope available to you. Write down the things the Holy Spirit is saying to you here.

Do

As the Holy Spirit speaks to you, make your confession to the Lord. Admit to Him those areas in your life where you have tried your best to cover your sins or the ways that you have tried to hide from Him. Ask Him to help you change your feelings and actions in those areas of your life and commit to obey His leading as you go forward from here.

Day 3

Knowledge and Blame

Searching the Scripture

Read Genesis 3:10-13:

> He answered, "I heard you in the Garden, and I was afraid because I was naked; so I hid." And he said, "Who told you that you were naked? Have you eaten from the tree that I commanded you not to eat from?" The man said, "The woman you put here with me—she gave me some fruit from the tree, and I ate it." Then the Lord God said to the woman, "What is this you have done?"
>
> The woman said, "The serpent deceived me, and I ate."

Answer the following questions:

- What was Adam's reaction to hearing God in the garden?

22 WEEK 1

- After Adam explained his reaction to God, what were the two questions that God asked in response?

- How did Adam answer God's question?

- What was Eve's response when God questioned her?

Yielding to the Spirit

Know

Adam and Eve were innocent prior to this event (compare what has happened with what the Scripture says in Genesis 2:25). Because they had been disobedient to God, they had become aware of things that God had not intended for them. They gained a distorted view of creation and the human body, because they had partaken of something that God had told them not to touch.

DAY 3: KNOWLEDGE AND BLAME 23

When God challenged Adam and Eve, their response was to shift the blame onto someone else. Adam blamed Eve, and Eve blamed the serpent. Another consequence of the fall is a failure to take personal responsibility. This is simply another form of fearfully hiding from God.

Be

Are there things that, through disobedience, you have been exposed to that were not God's will for you? Ask the Holy Spirit to reveal places in your life where you have been exposed to knowledge and experiences that God never intended you to have. Ask Him to reveal distorted perspectives you may have about the world and about other people. Confess these things to the Lord and ask Him to transform your mind as you pray, read His Word, and interact with His people. Also, are there some issues in your life for which you are not taking personal responsibility? Who have you blamed? Write anything the Holy Spirit may be saying to you here.

24 WEEK 1

Do

Think about the things the Holy Spirit has shown you today. Are there physical items in your environment you need to get rid of (publications, entertainment choices, etc.)? Are there some people you are in relationship with who are influencing you and exposing you to ungodly things? Pray and ask the Holy Spirit to guide you in how to handle these situations. If necessary, be willing to reconsider spending time with people that are hindering your growth as a person of the Spirit.

Day 4

Eden Lost

Searching the Scripture

Read Genesis 3:14-20:

> So the Lord God said to the serpent, "Because you have done this, Cursed are you above all livestock and all wild animals! You will crawl on your belly and you will eat dust all the days of your life. And I will put enmity between you and the woman, and between your offspring and hers; he will crush your head, and you will strike his heel.
>
> To the woman he said, "I will make your pains in childbearing very severe; with painful labor you will give birth to children. Your desire will be for your husband, and he will rule over you."
>
> To Adam he said, "Because you listened to your wife and ate fruit from the tree about which I commanded you, You must not eat from it, Cursed is the ground because of you; through painful toil you will eat food from it all the days of your life. It will produce thorns and thistles for you, and you will eat the plants of the field. By the sweat of your brow you will eat your food until you return to the ground, since from it you were

WEEK 1

taken; for dust you are and to dust you will return."

Adam named his wife Eve, because she would become the mother of all the living.

Answer the following questions:

- What is the result of God's judgment against the serpent?

- What is the twofold consequence promised to the woman as a result of the fall?

- What is the consequence pronounced upon Adam?

DAY 4: EDEN LOST 27

Yielding to the Spirit

Know

As a result of Adam and Eve's eating the fruit that God had told them not to eat, a curse was pronounced on God's good creation (to see how good creation was before the curse, read Genesis 1:1-31). The consequence of the first sin was tragic: a broken relationship with God, a broken relationship with one another, and a distorted relationship with creation. We see two out of three of these in today's reading:

- *Broken relationship with one another*—Eve had been given to complete Adam. They walked side by side in the garden, tending to it and ruling over it out of an unbroken relationship with the Creator (see Genesis 1:28). But, as a result of the fall, she would be ruled by her husband. In effect, instead of walking beside him, she would now walk behind him.

- *Distorted relationship with creation*—The work they had been given to do that was meant to be a joy had become a hardship. The woman would experience severe pain in childbirth as they fulfilled the

28 WEEK 1

mandate to be fruitful and multiply. Man's efforts to subdue the earth would be marked by painful toil and the sweat of his brow as he battled thorns and thistles in his quest for food, rather than loving care for the Garden of God.

Be

Sin still has these effects on us today individually and corporately as the human race. Think about how sin has complicated your life in ways that were obviously not what God intended for you. Also, think about how we are seeing the results of the fall still at work in the world:

- In relationships between men and women?
- In our care (or lack of care) for the environment?
- In our battle with nature for survival?

Ask the Holy Spirit to reveal thoughts and feelings in your life that are more like Genesis 3 than Genesis 1 and 2. Does your inner world (your thoughts, feelings, and desires) look more like God's good creation, or the chaos that came into play after the fall? Write down what the Holy Spirit is saying to you.

DAY 4: EDEN LOST

Do

Take a moment today to recommit yourself to the *People of the Spirit* process. In your prayer, ask the Lord to help you give the time and energy you spend on this study to Him as an offering. Ask the Holy Spirit to transform your thoughts and emotions as you work through this process. Ask God for His kingdom to come and His will be done in your inner world (thoughts, will, emotions).

30 WEEK 1

Day 5

A Glimmer of Hope

Searching the Scriptures

Read Genesis 3:21-24:

> The Lord God made garments of skin for Adam and his wife and clothed them. And the Lord God said, "The man has now become like one of us, knowing good and evil. He must not be allowed to reach out his hand and take also from the tree of life and eat, and live forever." So the Lord God banished him from the Garden of Eden to work the ground from which he had been taken. After he drove the man out, he placed on the east side of the Garden of Eden cherubim and a flaming sword flashing back and forth to guard the way to the tree of life.

Answer the following questions:

- What did God do in response to Adam and Eve's nakedness?

WEEK 1

- What would eating from the Tree of Life have done for Adam and Eve?

- What did God do to prevent Adam and Eve from eating from the Tree of Life?

Yielding to the Spirit

Know

Over the course of this week, you have closely looked at the Genesis account of the fall of humanity from the place of authority and dominion that had been given to them by God. What had once been a good creation was now subjected to a curse. The work that would have been a pleasure had now become drudgery. The joy of childbirth had been dampened by severe pain and trauma. The relationship between man and woman had been distorted and, in the days to come, women would be increasingly treated as not much better than property.

But biblical scholars have seen something else in these verses—they see signs of hope and redemption. Hidden in these words is a clue that God's mercy will prevail.

DAY 5: A GLIMER OF HOPE 33

We see this in a phrase from yesterday's reading and a divine action in today's reading.

In Genesis 3:15, God tells the serpent that the offspring of the woman will one day crush the serpent's head, and all the serpent will be able to do with him is strike his feet. Is it possible that someone will be born of a woman (without an earthly father perhaps?) that will finally conquer evil completely and save us all?

In today's reading in Genesis 3:21, there is another clue. When God made garments of animal skin for Adam and Eve, some say it points to the animal sacrifices for Israel's sin that will be taught by Moses. Some also say that it points to Jesus Christ, the ultimate sacrifice for sin, resulting in salvation for all who will receive it.

But for now, we see here in the story that humanity has left the garden. The words of the serpent have fallen to the ground. They will no longer be able to eat from the Tree of Life. They will continue to exist outside of the garden, but it will only be a shadow of the life they had known inside it. The full effects of the sin have been realized—ultimately, they will physically die. But immediately, they have experienced separation from God, with all entrances to the garden blocked by angels with flaming swords.

WEEK 1

Be

Take time to meditate on God's perspective of these events. How do you think God felt as His good creation was subjected to a curse because Adam and Eve had disobeyed a simple instruction? What do you think these words of hope say about His character? Why would God take action to save these people who have done this? Write your thoughts below.

Do

Take time to thank God for the fact that He did not abandon His creation. Think about what it would mean for you to offer yourself to Him as a participant in His planned rescue. Ask the Holy Spirit to help you become willing to be used by God in this way.

Week 2

Day 1

The Call of Abraham

Learning the Story

In the beginning was God. Everything God created was good, and that includes the culmination of His creation—Adam and Eve. They were made in His image. They were given the responsibility to care for the creation on His behalf. They walked with Him daily and out of an unbroken relationship with Him, they perfectly reflected His glory in the Garden of Eden. They were totally

36 WEEK 2

submitted to Him in every way, and all creation benefitted from that relationship.

Then the serpent deceived Eve, and Eve gave the forbidden fruit to Adam. In one moment, with one decision, Adam and Eve usurped the authority of the Lord of all, and everything that had been so perfect, so pristine, so *right*, was now something else entirely.

What about God? What about His righteousness? What about His good creation? Would He just stand by and watch it decay into a sea of chaos and despair? It doesn't take long to get our answer. Before they are even forced to leave the garden, God makes a statement to the serpent that leaves us wondering and maybe even hopeful that one day justice will reign . . .

> And I will put enmity between you and the woman, and between your offspring and hers; he will crush your head, and you will strike his heel (Genesis 3:15).

Even though the serpent will strike his heel, the offspring of the woman will crush his head. But . . . the offspring of the woman? Such a strange choice of words. What about the child's father? Who will he be?

DAY 1: THE CALL OF ABRAHAM   37

With those questions left unanswered for the time being, Adam and Eve left the garden and began to live their lives, dealing with the consequences of their actions. They could never go back because an angel with a flaming sword blocked the entrance. There was nowhere to go but forward.

Centuries passed and the human race continued its descent into chaos and evil—so much so that God moved to destroy everything except a small remnant that was saved in an ark built by a man named Noah, who found grace in the eyes of the Lord (Genesis 6:8 NKJV). Eventually God came to a man named Abram and promised to raise up a special people group from his descendants. There was only one problem—Abram and his wife Sarai (God later changed their names to Abraham and Sarah) had no children together and they were very old and past the normal time for this to happen. But God performed a miracle and gave them a son in their old age. His name was Isaac. Later, Isaac had two sons—Jacob and Esau. Jacob had twelve sons who became the leaders of the special people promised by God. They became the nation of Israel. It would be through the people of Israel that God would once again begin to reveal Himself to humanity. The

WEEK 2

story of Israel is what the Old Testament is all about—and it is part of our story too. Everything that you have read so far is recorded in the Book of Genesis.

Jacob and his sons moved to Egypt to escape a famine, and over the years became very prosperous there. They became a threat to the Pharaoh and so were forced into slavery. They stayed there for several hundred years until God called a man named Moses to lead them out. But this exodus only took place after many plagues struck the land of Egypt, ending up in the loss of the firstborn of every household. The only exception to this loss were those who obeyed the Lord's instructions to prepare a special meal, including a lamb, and to put the blood of the lamb on the doorpost of their homes. This meal became known as the Passover. This story is recorded in the Bible in the Book of Exodus.

By this time, Israel was made up of a large group of people. As God brought them out of Egypt, He worked miracles, including crossing the Red Sea on dry ground and giving them manna (a type of bread) that fell from heaven to feed them. In the process, God gave them His law to teach them what it looked like for them to be His special people. The Law contained Ten Commandments that

DAY 1: THE CALL OF ABRAHAM 39

talked about how they should honor God and honor one another (you can read these in Exodus 20). God gave Israel many other instructions. Because He knew that they would not be able to do all of these things flawlessly, He also gave them a sacrificial system so that they would know how to seek Him for forgiveness when they fell short of obeying His law.

Searching the Scripture

Read Genesis 12:1-3:

> The Lord had said to Abram, "Go from your country, your people and your father's household to the land I will show you. I will make you into a great nation, and I will bless you; I will make your name great, and you will be a blessing. I will bless those who bless you, and whoever curses you I will curse; and all peoples on earth will be blessed through you."

Answer the following questions:

- What was Abraham's duty in this covenant?

40 WEEK 2

- What did God promise to do in exchange for Abraham's obedience?

- As a result of Abraham's obedience and God's action, what would Abraham eventually become?

- How many people would ultimately benefit from Abraham's obedience?

Yielding to the Spirit

Know

Christians rightly understand this passage to be a prophetic statement about Jesus Christ, the Son of God, the Messiah of Israel, and the Savior of the world. In His earthly lineage, He would physically descend from Abraham, and, through Him, all people groups on the earth are

DAY 1: THE CALL OF ABRAHAM   41

blessed. As we will see in the days ahead, Israel's story is about the way being made for the coming of Jesus at the fullness of time (Galatians 4:4). But even before His coming and now while we are waiting on Him to return, the descendants of Abraham (physical and spiritual) have been and continue to be a blessing to all peoples of the earth.

In order for all of this to happen, Abraham was first called to leave his home and family and go to a place that was totally unfamiliar to him. He didn't have the full picture when God called him out, but he responded faithfully over and over again. Therefore, Abraham's faithful response to the word of the Lord was credited to him as righteousness (Gen. 15:6; Rom. 4:3).

As a son or daughter of Abraham (by faith), your story is connected with his. Reflect on your own experiences with God. Have you heard the Lord telling you to simply follow Him even though He hasn't told you all the details about where you are going or what you will do when you get there? Have you obeyed Him? How has God blessed you as a result?

WEEK 2

Be

It must have been a challenging decision for Abraham to decide to obey the call of God on his life. He had to leave familiar surroundings and familiar people to go somewhere he had never been. And all of this was as a result of a God that he had not known up until that time. Thankfully for all of us, Abraham was obedient.

What about you? Are there areas in your life where you have not obediently responded to God? Are there things you are doing that He called you to stop doing? Are there things you are *not* doing that He has called you to *start* doing? How would your faithful response to the Lord's invitation to follow Him result in a blessing for those around you in your family, church, community, and in the world? Take a few moments and ask the Holy Spirit to show you these things. Write them down here, then confess them to the Lord and ask Him to forgive you for not being fully obedient to His call on your life to follow Him.

DAY 1: THE CALL OF ABRAHAM · 43

Do

As a result of the previous question, what are some practical changes that need to be made in your life? Take a moment to write down two or three things that you feel led to do to take some practical steps toward faithful obedience to the Lord's call to follow Him. Prayerfully ask the Holy Spirit how to proceed to the next step from here and commit to obey His leading.

44 WEEK 2

Day 2

Exodus From Egypt

Searching the Scripture

Read Exodus 14:10-28:

As Pharaoh approached, the Israelites looked up, and there were the Egyptians, marching after them. They were terrified and cried out to the Lord. They said to Moses, "Was it because there were no graves in Egypt that you brought us to the desert to die? What have you done to us by bringing us out of Egypt? Didn't we say to you in Egypt, 'Leave us alone; let us serve the Egyptians'? It would have been better for us to serve the Egyptians than to die in the desert!"

Moses answered the people, "Do not be afraid. Stand firm and you will see the deliverance the Lord will bring you today. The Egyptians you see today you will never see again. The Lord will fight for you; you need only to be still."

Then the Lord said to Moses, "Why are you crying out to me? Tell the Israelites to move on. Raise your staff and stretch out your hand over the sea to divide the water so that the Israelites can go through the sea on

46 WEEK 2

dry ground. I will harden the hearts of the Egyptians so that they will go in after them. And I will gain glory through Pharaoh and all his army, through his chariots and his horsemen. The Egyptians will know that I am the Lord when I gain glory through Pharaoh, his chariots and his horsemen."

Then the angel of God, who had been traveling in front of Israel's army, withdrew and went behind them. The pillar of cloud also moved from in front and stood behind them, coming between the armies of Egypt and Israel. Throughout the night the cloud brought darkness to the one side and light to the other side; so neither went near the other all night long.

Then Moses stretched out his hand over the sea, and all that night the Lord drove the sea back with a strong east wind and turned it into dry land. The waters were divided, and the Israelites went through the sea on dry ground, with a wall of water on their right and on their left.

The Egyptians pursued them, and all Pharaoh's horses and chariots and horsemen followed them into the sea. During the last watch of the night the Lord looked down from the pillar of fire and cloud at the Egyptian army and threw it into confusion. He jammed the wheels of their chariots so that they had difficulty driving. And the Egyptians said, "Let's get away from the Israelites! The Lord is fighting for them against Egypt."

DAY 2: EXODUS FROM EGYPT 47

Then the Lord said to Moses, "Stretch out your hand over the sea so that the waters may flow back over the Egyptians and their chariots and horsemen." Moses stretched out his hand over the sea, and at daybreak the sea went back to its place. The Egyptians were fleeing toward it, and the Lord swept them into the sea. The water flowed back and covered the chariots and horsemen—the entire army of Pharaoh that had followed the Israelites into the sea. Not one of them survived.

Answer the following questions:

- What were the Israelites saying as they saw Pharaoh approaching them from behind? (vv. 10-12)

- What was Moses' answer to the Israelites? (vv. 13-14)

- What were the Lord's instructions to the Israelites in the face of the threat from Pharaoh's army?

48 **WEEK 2**

- Look closely at verses 17-18, exactly who do we see performing the action here? What appears to be the goal of the action?

- What did God do in this incident that led Israel to safety? What became of Pharaoh's army?

Yielding to the Spirit

Know

After the plagues struck Egypt and the Israelites were finally released, God Himself led them to this place on the banks of the Red Sea. The Scripture says, "the Lord went ahead of them in a pillar of cloud to guide them on their way and by night in a pillar of fire to give them light, so that they could travel by day or by night" (Ex. 13:21-22). This wasn't a case of Moses losing his way and misleading the Israelites. This is an example of a time when the Lord

DAY 2: EXODUS FROM EGYPT   49

led them right to a place that was going to test their faith in Him.

From reading verses 17-18, we can see the reason for this chain of events. The Israelites were slaves of the Egyptians. They had forgotten their calling as descendants of Abraham (remember your Day 1 encounter this week). At the same time, the Egyptians looked to Pharaoh as a god. It is possible that their misplaced worship had confused the Israelites as well. But God led them to this place to deliver His people by His own hand. He declared as a result of His actions on this day, "I will gain glory through Pharaoh and all his army . . . the Egyptians will know that I am the Lord" (Ex. 14:4).

Be

Allow the Holy Spirit to speak to you about circumstances you (or perhaps your family or church) are facing that seem to be confusing and hopeless. What has been your attitude during this season? Have you been like the Israelites who were terrified and were ready to give up and go back into slavery? Or are you like Moses who called to the Israelites to "Stand firm and . . . see the deliverance the Lord will bring you today?" Are you willing to follow

50 WEEK 2

the Lord through good times and bad times in order to see your faith strengthened and for the Lord to gain glory in your eyes and the eyes of those who are watching your life? Write what the Holy Spirit is saying to you here.

Do

When you meet with your discipleship partner this week, take some time to share and discuss the things you have written about today. Remember to allow him/her to share their stories too. Then pray for one another. You might consider using Jesus' words to Peter in Luke 22 as a model for how you should pray for them (note especially the underlined phrases):

> Simon, Simon, Satan has asked to sift all of you as wheat. But I have prayed for you, Simon, that your faith may not fail. And when you have turned back, strengthen your brothers (Luke 22:31–32).

Day 3

A Holy People

Searching the Scripture

Read Exodus 19:1-8:

> On the first day of the third month after the Israelites left Egypt—on that very day—they came to the Desert of Sinai. After they set out from Rephidim, they entered the Desert of Sinai, and Israel camped there in the desert in front of the mountain. Then Moses went up to God, and the Lord called to him from the mountain and said, "This is what you are to say to the descendants of Jacob and what you are to tell the people of Israel: 'You yourselves have seen what I did to Egypt, and how I carried you on eagles' wings and brought you to myself. Now if you obey me fully and keep my covenant, then out of all nations you will be my treasured possession. Although the whole earth is mine, you will be for me a kingdom of priests and a holy nation.' These are the words you are to speak to the Israelites."

> So Moses went back and summoned the elders of the people and set before them all the words the Lord had commanded him

52 WEEK 2

to speak. The people all responded together, "We will do everything the Lord has said." So Moses brought their answer back to the Lord.

Answer the following questions:

- What had God done to reveal Himself to the people of Israel as their powerful God?

- What did God ask Israel to do?

- Into what was God wanting to make Israel?

- What was Israel's response?

Yielding to the Spirit

Know

God had called Abraham, but that had been centuries before. Now He was revealing Himself powerfully once again to Abraham's descendants, the people of Israel, in

DAY 3: A HOLY PEOPLE 53

His act of delivering them from slavery in Egypt, as well as from Pharaoh's army. But God did not just do this as an act of mercy—He had a plan for them. They were going to be a kingdom of priests, a holy nation, set apart for His purposes. In other words, they would be priestly in the sense that they would act as a link between the rest of the world and God in order to bring them back together. Furthermore, they were a holy people. God had delivered them from Egyptian bondage and now they were His possession, dedicated to Him alone.

The same can be said of each of us who have been saved from guilt and set free from the bondage of sin. Peter wrote very similar words about us:

> But you are a chosen people, a royal priesthood, a holy nation, God's special possession, that you may declare the praises of him who called you out of darkness into his wonderful light. Once you were not a people, but now you are the people of God; once you had not received mercy, but now you have received mercy (1 Peter 2:9–10).

Be

Take some time to consider your salvation story. What was your life like before you became part of God's family through faith in Jesus? Out of what kinds of things

54 WEEK 2

did God deliver you? What part do you play in the people who are called to declare the praises of the Lord? You were saved *from* something and saved *to* something.

Do

You are called in some way to faithfully declare the praises of the Lord who saved you and to invite others into a life of following Him as well. What are some things in your life that may be holding you back from fully walking in your calling? Write them down in the space below, and then take some time to pray and ask the Lord to forgive you for anything that has been more important to you than engaging in God's mission. Prayerfully consider how God may be calling you to participate in what He is doing in the world around you, bringing people to Him for salvation.

Day 4

The Problem with Idols

Searching the Scripture

Read Exodus 32:1-8:

> When the people saw that Moses was so long
> in coming down from the mountain, they
> gathered around Aaron and said, "Come,
> make us gods who will go before us. As for
> this fellow Moses who brought us up out of
> Egypt, we don't know what has happened to
> him." Aaron answered them, "Take off the
> gold earrings that your wives, your sons and
> your daughters are wearing, and bring them
> to me." So all the people took off their ear-
> rings and brought them to Aaron. He took
> what they handed him and made it into an
> idol cast in the shape of a calf, fashioning it
> with a tool. Then they said, "These are your
> gods, Israel, who brought you up out of
> Egypt." When Aaron saw this, he built an altar
> in front of the calf and announced, "Tomor-
> row there will be a festival to the Lord." So
> the next day the people rose early and sacri-
> ficed burnt offerings and presented fellow-
> ship offerings. Afterward they sat down to eat
> and drink and got up to indulge in revelry.
> Then the Lord said to Moses, "Go down, be-
> cause your people, whom you brought up out

WEEK 2

of Egypt, have become corrupt. They have been quick to turn away from what I commanded them and have made themselves an idol cast in the shape of a calf. They have bowed down to it and sacrificed to it and have said, 'These are your gods, Israel, who brought you up out of Egypt.'

Answer the following questions:

- Why did the Israelites get restless and approach Aaron about making another god?

- Into what shape did they make the idol?

- Describe the worship they gave to this idol.

Yielding to the Spirit

Know

God's intention was to separate Israel out from the rest of the people groups in the world to make them His

DAY 4: THE PROBLEM WITH IDOLS 57

own special people. They were to be sanctified (set apart and made holy) for His purposes. Israel accepted God's offer, and God called Moses up to the mountain where He would give Moses the law that would govern the people of Israel morally (their behavior), socially (their relationships), and spiritually (their worship of God).

The incident we have read today took place while Moses was on the mountain with God. Moses had been on the mountain with God for a long time—long enough that the people of Israel became restless and approached Moses' brother, Aaron, asking him to fashion a god for them to worship. Aaron agreed and used the gold jewelry belonging to the people to make an idol in the shape of a calf. The people were pleased and declared, "these are your gods, Israel, who brought you up out of Egypt" (Ex. 32:4).

The worship of this golden calf started out simple enough, with burnt offerings. But it quickly descended into a time of pleasing their own sensual desires as they indulged in revelry. Their sinful idolatry resulted in great loss of life by sword and by plague (see Ex. 32:25-35).

Be

It is easy to become discouraged when God doesn't act as quickly, or in the same manner, as we think He should. In those times, we are tempted to take matters into our own hands. For example, we are tempted to not do things the Lord's way and pursue a path that makes more sense to our natural mind. It is all too easy to excuse our actions, or to even deceive ourselves into believing that what we are doing is God's will. But the truth is, when we consciously decide to live life and handle situations in a way that is unbiblical and un-Christlike, we become guilty of idolatry, just like the children of Israel. In a way, we have fashioned a god for ourselves that seems more familiar, and who will allow us to live and do things in a way that makes us more comfortable. Just like it was for the Israelites, the end result will ultimately be costly and destructive.

Allow the Holy Spirit to speak to you right now about your life. Have there been times when you have grown impatient with God's timing or will and chose to do things in a way that made you feel better? What kind of idol did you fashion for yourself to defend your actions? Did you try to use religious behavior or even selected Bible

DAY 4: THE PROBLEM WITH IDOLS 59

verses to justify yourself? What was the end result? Write your thoughts here.

Do

If you have not already done so, take this time to repent for idolatry that the Holy Spirit has made you aware of during your encounter today. Perhaps the Holy Spirit is speaking to you about some practical steps you need to take as a result of your repentance. Is there a confession that needs to be made to someone? Do you need to make restitution? Use the space below to write anything that comes to mind. You may want to discuss these with your discipleship partner for support, encouragement, and accountability.

60 WEEK 2

Day 5

An Important Decision

Searching the Scripture

Read Deuteronomy 30:15-20:

> See, I set before you today life and prosperity, death and destruction. For I command you today to love the Lord your God, to walk in obedience to him, and to keep his commands, decrees and laws; then you will live and increase, and the Lord your God will bless you in the land you are entering to possess.

> But if your heart turns away and you are not obedient, and if you are drawn away to bow down to other gods and worship them, I declare to you this day that you will certainly be destroyed. You will not live long in the land you are crossing the Jordan to enter and possess.

> This day I call the heavens and the earth as witnesses against you that I have set before you life and death, blessings and curses. Now choose life, so that you and your children may live and that you may love the Lord your God, listen to his voice, and hold fast to him. For the Lord is your life, and he will give you

62 WEEK 2

many years in the land he swore to give to your fathers, Abraham, Isaac and Jacob.

Answer the following questions:

- What are the options being set before the Israelites?

- What does Moses command them to do?

- What will be the result if they obey?

- What will be the result if they do not obey?

Yielding to the Spirit

Know

This text is part of Moses' farewell address to the people of Israel. After 40 years of wilderness wandering, they are finally about to occupy the Promised Land and he will no longer be with them. They will have to choose whether they will continue to live in obedience to God's

DAY 5: AN IMPORTANT DECISION   63

commandments and instructions or choose to live life in a way that seemed right to them. The consequences of the decision are clear—life and prosperity or death and destruction. Which will they choose? If they want to continue to live in the Promised Land, there is only one option—obedience to God.

During the 40 years in the wilderness, God provided water and food for the Israelites. Their clothes and shoes didn't wear out. He led them where He wanted them to go by a pillar of fire at night and a cloud by day. But everything would change when they came into the Promised Land. They would have to drive out the occupants of the land. The manna would stop once they started eating the produce of the land. They would eventually begin to establish stable lives. They would start businesses and build homes. They would be expected to mature and grow and represent the kingdom of God to all the nations of the earth.

Be

We too must come to a place of productivity in the kingdom of God. All too often, however, people prefer to wander around the wilderness circling the same mountain

WEEK 2

over and over again, never breaking through to new levels of depth and maturity. We eventually are called to make the same decision as the people of Israel— are we going to serve God and live life His way, or are we going to do it our way? Be careful how you choose, because ultimately the consequences are the same as they were then.

In the New Testament, James wrote these words:

> If any of you lacks wisdom, you should ask God, who gives generously to all without finding fault, and it will be given to you. But when you ask, you must believe and not doubt, because the one who doubts is like a wave of the sea, blown and tossed by the wind. That person should not expect to receive anything from the Lord. Such a person is double-minded and unstable in all they do (James 1:5-8).

Have you been guilty of being double-minded and unstable when it comes to doing the Lord's will? Are there days when you are obedient and days when you are not? Ask the Holy Spirit to reveal the truth and to help you not be deceived.

Do

In your prayer time today, ask the Holy Spirit to sanctify you. This means that you are not only set apart as God's child, but that you are being transformed into the

DAY 5: AN IMPORTANT DECISION 65

kind of person who wants with all their heart to live life in a way that pleases God. Trust God as He teaches you new ways to perceive the world, including your relationships with other people.

66 WEEK 2

Week 3

Day 1

No Other Gods

Learning the Story

Before we go forward in the story, we first need to go backward. This week, we are going to travel back to the mountain where God called Israel out to be His special people.

It had been quite a journey out of Egypt. The Israelites had seen God bring them through the crossing of the Red Sea (Ex. 14:10-31)—a miracle that also delivered them from Egyptian armies who were coming to take them back to their slavery. The Lord had sweetened the bitter waters of Marah (Ex. 15:22-25), supernaturally sent manna and quail to feed them when they were hungry

68 WEEK 3

(Ex. 16:1-15), provided water from a rock at Rephidim (Ex. 17:1-7), and delivered them from the armies of Amalek (Ex. 17:8-16).

Now, a little over two months later, God had brought the Israelites to Mount Sinai. This is the place where they became tired of waiting on God and built a golden calf. God had given Moses two tablets of stone during his time on the mountain, and as a result of seeing Israel's sin, Moses threw the tablets down, breaking them into pieces at the foot of the mountain (Ex. 32:19). So God told Moses to chisel out two more stone tablets and on them He would write the words that He had written on the first tablets, which Moses had broken (Ex. 34:1). "And he wrote on the tablets the words of the covenant—the Ten Commandments" (Ex. 34:28).

A covenant, by definition, is a way of establishing a relationship where one does not naturally exist, and is sanctioned by an oath sworn in a ceremony of ratification.[2] In this case, Israel, as we have already seen, had been

---

[2] William Sanford Lasor, David Allan Hubbard, and Frederic William Bush, *Old Testament Survey: The Message, Form, and Background of the Old Testament*, 2nd ed.(Grand Rapids, MI: Wm. B. Eerdman's Publishing Co., 1996), p. 73.

DAY 1: NO OTHER GODS 69

called to be the special people of God—"a kingdom of priests and a holy nation" (Ex. 19:6). This was going to require them to be a unique sort of people. They would be called upon to live their lives in keeping with the nature of the One they were going to represent to the world. The Ten Commandments were not written in the form of law. That would be done later in the Book of Exodus and spelled out further in the rest of the Torah. But they were a basic statement of the kind of behavior that would be expected of this special group of people called to be a kingdom of priests.[3] The Ten Commandments still represent characteristics of God's people to this day.

Searching the Scripture

Read Exodus 20:1-7:

> God spoke all these words: "I am the Lord your God, who brought you out of Egypt, out of the land of slavery. You shall have no other gods before me. You shall not make for yourself an image in the form of anything in heaven above or on the earth beneath or in the waters below. You shall not bow down to them or worship them; for I, the Lord your God, am a jealous God, punishing the children for the sin of the parents to the third and

---

[3] Ibid., p. 75.

WEEK 3

fourth generation of those who hate me, but showing love to a thousand generations of those who love me and keep my commandments. You shall not misuse the name of the Lord your God, for the Lord will not hold anyone guiltless who misuses his name."

Answer the following questions:

- How does God describe Himself to the people of Israel at the beginning of the passage?

- What are the three things the Israelites are told not to do in this passage?

- What word does God use to describe Himself to the Israelites after the statements prohibiting idol worship?

- What are the consequences promised to those who hate God?

DAY 1: NO OTHER GODS   71

- What are the blessings promised to those who love God and keep His commandments?

- What does God say about those who misuse His name?

Yielding to the Spirit

Know

This passage contains the first three of the Ten Commandments. In the first commandment, God declares Himself to be Israel's one and only God from the start and declares that there are to be no other gods as the object of their worship. The second commandment is that the Israelites are not to make any kind of image and then offer worship to it. The third commandment is that they are to be careful about how they use the name of God. Carelessly misusing God's name will certainly result in punishment.

With all the choices and distractions available to us today, it is easy to put our relationship with the Lord at the back of our mind. Certainly a part of us still serves God, but

WEEK 3

it is not consuming too much of our time, talent, or treasure. However, when we read this portion of the Ten Commandments, we see that there is no place for God's special people to be casual about their relationship with Him. We are to remember that it was He—and no other—who saved us from sin and its bondage. No one can take His place in our lives. We cannot casually use the name Christian or thoughtlessly throw up prayers in Jesus' name if we are going to honor God in the way that He demands. Our love for God will result in being totally committed to Him, and will accept no substitutes. As a result, our children and families will be blessed. But if we hate God (in other words, fail to love Him with all our heart, mind, soul, and strength), the consequences could impact our family for generations.

Be

Several things could signal a casual devotion to God as our Lord: being casual about consistent and energetic participation in your church; being inconsistent about prayer, reading, and obeying God's Word; just to name a few. Ask the Holy Spirit to show you if your devotion to God has become casual in any way. Has God become just

DAY 1: NO OTHER GODS 73

one of many other things/people to whom you give your loyalty through the use of your time, talent, and treasure? What are some other gods that you have set before Him? Write what the Holy Spirit is saying to you here.

Do

Without delay, confess to the Lord how and where you have become casual in your devotion to Him. Ask Him for strength to repent for wrong thinking and acting. Be prepared today to obey His direction in practical ways without hesitating.

74 WEEK 3

Day 2

Remember the Sabbath

Searching the Scripture

Read Exodus 20:8-11:

> Remember the Sabbath day by keeping it holy. Six days you shall labor and do all your work, but the seventh day is a sabbath to the Lord your God. On it you shall not do any work, neither you, nor your son or daughter, nor your male or female servant, nor your animals, nor any foreigner residing in your towns. For in six days the Lord made the heavens and the earth, the sea, and all that is in them, but he rested on the seventh day. Therefore the Lord blessed the Sabbath day and made it holy.

Answer the following questions:

- How are the Israelites told to remember the Sabbath day?

76 WEEK 3

- When are they supposed to labor and do all their work?

- What are they told to do on the Sabbath?

- What explanation does God give for this command?

Yielding to the Spirit

Know

This passage contains the fourth of the Ten Commandments, "Remember the Sabbath day by keeping it holy." This is similar to the previous three commandments in that it has to do with the proper worship of Israel's one true God. God did not give them the opportunity to decide *how* they wanted to worship Him. He immediately began

DAY 2: REMEMBER THE SABBATH 77

to give instructions in this area. Because of that, this commandment is different from the first three in that it is telling them something *to do* instead of something *not to do.*

The Israelites are told to keep the Sabbath day holy by resting from all their labor. This command is both moral and ceremonial. It is moral because it is meant to require that God's special people set aside a dedicated time to worship and serve God. It is ceremonial in that the Israelites were instructed to do this on the seventh day. However the Church changed the ceremonial requirement of that day from the seventh day to the first day in recognition of God's new deliverance of His people accomplished in the death and resurrection of Jesus that was finally accomplished on the first day.[4]

The command to honor the Sabbath is still relevant to God's people today. It is a reminder that we are to set aside a specific time to stop what we are doing to focus on the worship of God. It reminds us that the weight of the world is not on our shoulders, but is upon His. We put our trust and dependence in Him, and we demonstrate that dependence in this practical way. We surrender ourselves

---

[4] Walter C. Kaiser, "Exodus," in *The Expositor's Bible Commentary: Genesis-Leviticus*, eds. David E. Garland and Tremper Longman III (Grand Rapids, MI: Zondervan, 2008), p. 482.

WEEK 3

to the worship of, and dependence upon, God rather than the tyranny of our demanding schedules.

Be

Ask the Holy Spirit to speak to you about your use of time. It has been said that our calendars are statements that reveal what we truly believe about God. What does your calendar say about you? Have you prioritized regular time with God each day? Have you prioritized a day of the week where you worship God with His people and take time to physically rest and recuperate? If the answer to these questions is no, then how has that affected you emotionally, physically and spiritually? Write your thoughts here.

Do

Recommit yourself today to prioritizing God on your calendar, including daily time with Him and commitment to gathering together with God's people for corpo-

DAY 2: REMEMBER THE SABBATH 79

rate worship on a consistent basis. If you need to have a conversation with someone to accomplish this—your spouse, your children, your employer, etc.—then begin the process needed to have that conversation today.

80 WEEK 3

Day 3

Right Relationships

Searching the Scripture

Read Exodus 20:12-17:

> Honor your father and your mother, so that you may live long in the land the Lord your God is giving you. You shall not murder. You shall not commit adultery. You shall not steal. You shall not give false testimony against your neighbor. You shall not covet your neighbor's house. You shall not covet your neighbor's wife, or his male or female servant, his ox or donkey, or anything that belongs to your neighbor.

Answer the following questions:

- How are we supposed to relate to our father and mother?

82 WEEK 3

- Why are we supposed to relate to them in this way?

- What other things does this passage tell us not to do?

Yielding to the Spirit

Know

This passage contains the last six of the Ten Commandments. Notice that the first four were related directly to the Israelites' relationship with God. These six, however, specifically deal with their relationships with one another. This reveals something important about what it means to be God's special people: how we interact with other people is just as important as how we relate to God. The two cannot be separated.

Some Christians seem to think that as long as they have good doctrine, that their relationship with other people is not important. But the truth is, good doctrine will

DAY 3: RIGHT RELATIONSHIPS   83

lead to right relationships with others. Those others are to include our family, our fellow believers, and those who have not yet become part of God's family. As a matter of fact, this is such a huge thing for God that Jesus told us that it was what identified us as belonging to Him when He said, "By this everyone will know that you are my disciples, if you love one another" (John 13:35).

Be

It is not enough to be a faithful disciple of the Lord, having just a private relationship with Him. The Lord expects you to maintain right relationships with others. Ask the Holy Spirit to speak to your heart about your relationships with other people. What is your attitude toward the church? Are you critical? Are you unforgiving toward those that may have offended you? What about your family? Does your relationship with them bring honor to the One you profess to follow? Write your thoughts here.

84 WEEK 3

Do

In your prayer today, be attentive to the leading of the Holy Spirit. Take any practical steps you feel you need to take to strengthen relationships with others. Sometimes a kind word or gesture is all that is needed. In other cases, a visit, a phone call, or an email is in order. When you meet with your discipleship peer this week, talk about this with him/her. Pray together about how the Lord may be leading you in this area of your relationship with Him.

Day 4

Reverent Fear

Searching the Scripture

Read Exodus 20:18-21:

> When the people saw the thunder and lightning and heard the trumpet and saw the mountain in smoke, they trembled with fear. They stayed at a distance and said to Moses, "Speak to us yourself and we will listen. But do not have God speak to us or we will die." Moses said to the people, "Do not be afraid. God has come to test you, so that the fear of God will be with you to keep you from sinning." The people remained at a distance, while Moses approached the thick darkness where God was.

Answer the following questions:

- The thunder, lightning, and loud trumpet sounds the Israelites heard are known as a *theophany* which is, "an appearance of God that is perceptible

WEEK 3

to human sight."[5] How did the Israelites respond to this theophany?

- What did the Israelites ask Moses to do for them?

- Why did they ask him to do this?

- Why did God come to test them?

Yielding to the Spirit

Know

The word "fear" used in this text is another word for reverence. It is the same word that was used later in a Proverb that says, "the fear of the Lord is the beginning of wisdom" (Proverbs 9:10). When Moses told them that God

---

[5] Donald K. McKim, "Theophany," in *Westminster Dictionary of Theological Terms*, ed. Donald K. McKim Louisville, KY: Westminster John Knox Press, 1996).

DAY 4: REVERENT FEAR   87

was testing them, it simply meant God was proving to them through their experience something that He already knew about them.[6] And what He knew was this—their reverence for Him helped to keep them from violating his commandments. In other words, their fear of God caused them to live wisely.

One more thing needs to be said here. After hearing these Ten Commandments, the Israelites were struck by their need for someone to go between them and God and act as a mediator. We will follow up on that thought in to-morrow's daily encounter.

Be

Ask the Holy Spirit to speak to you about your reverence for the Lord. Are you too casual about your relationship with Him? (See Day 1 of this week for a discussion on that topic.) Has there been any area of your life—your thoughts, actions, or relationships—where you have not been living in reverence to God or allowing Him to lead you? Have your communication, entertainment choices,

---

[6] Kaiser, "Exodus," p. 485.

WEEK 3

and your sense of humor been irreverent toward Him? Write your thoughts here.

Do

Be honest with God about things the Holy Spirit is showing you. Remember that 1 John 1:9 says, "If we confess our sins, he is faithful and just and will forgive us our sins and purify us from all unrighteousness." Make a fresh commitment to be led by the Holy Spirit and demonstrate that commitment in practical, concrete changes in light of the above insights.

Day 5

That Prophet

Searching the Scripture

Read Deuteronomy 18:15-19:

> The Lord your God will raise up for you a prophet like me from among you, from your fellow Israelites. You must listen to him. For this is what you asked of the Lord your God at Horeb on the day of the assembly when you said, "Let us not hear the voice of the Lord our God nor see this great fire anymore, or we will die." The Lord said to me: "What they say is good. I will raise up for them a prophet like you from among their fellow Israelites, and I will put my words in his mouth. He will tell them everything I command him. I myself will call to account anyone who does not listen to my words that the prophet speaks in my name."

Answer the following questions:

- What is God going to raise up for the Israelites?

90 WEEK 3

- Why is He going to do this?

- What is God going to put in that prophet's mouth?

- What will that prophet do?

- What will God do to anyone who does not listen to His words that the prophet speaks in His name?

Yielding to the Spirit

Know

Yesterday we read about the reaction of the Israelites to the theophany in Exodus 20. After hearing the commands of the Lord and seeing the awesome display of His power, they responded by telling Moses to go and speak to God on their behalf. They knew they needed

DAY 5: THAT PROPHET 91

someone to be a go-between, or mediator, between them and God. On that day, that mediator was Moses. The passage you are reading today refers to that episode. God heard what the Israelites said and agreed with it. The Israelites were correct in saying they needed someone to speak to God on their behalf. So here we see a prophecy about One who would emerge from Israel and in whose mouth God would put His words. Many biblical scholars agree that this is a reference to the first coming of Jesus that is revealed in the Gospels. From the very beginning, God's special people knew they needed a mediator. But it would be a long process of struggle and waiting before He would finally come.

Be

This week's study has focused on the characteristics that God expects of His people. At times, the teachings of Scripture can seem overwhelming to us, just like God's words and power were for Israel. The call to forgive those who have hurt us, to love our enemies, and to fully trust and obey God can be challenging and even upsetting at times. But God has made it possible for us to be changed into holy people because of the ministry of Jesus Christ—

92 WEEK 3

the ultimate fulfillment of Moses' prophecy in today's text. Take a moment to reflect on your experience thus far with God. How have you reacted to His presence in your life? Have you run away from Him in fear of what He might say to you or ask you to do? Or have you accepted the grace and mercy He has offered you through His Son?

Do

Pray this prayer of confession and surrender to the Lord:

Father, I confess to You that I am powerless to become the person that You intended for me to be. I confess that I have hidden from You because of fear of how You might see me, or of what You might say to me. I confess to You that, like the people of God in Deuteronomy, I stand in need of someone to help me, to bring me into Your presence. I need the ministry of Your Son, Jesus, who came to fulfill Moses' prophecy. I will listen to the words that He speaks and do what He tells me to do.

Week 4

Day 1

David's Throne

Learning the Story

With the call of God upon their lives to be a kingdom of priests and a holy nation, the Israelites moved forward under the leadership of Joshua to conquer the land of Canaan. With some setbacks and many victories, they were able to eventually occupy the land that God had promised so long ago to Abraham. For a time, the people lived without any kind of organized structure. When needed, God would raise up judges (military leaders) to deliver them from their enemies—people like Samson, Deborah, and

94 WEEK 4

Gideon whose stories are recorded in the Book of Judges. But eventually, the people decided they wanted a king.

Although each is significant in his own way, the most important one for our story is David. David was said to be a man after God's own heart (1 Samuel 13:14). Although David had his flaws, he was a true worshiper and laid the plans for building a temple for the Lord. Later the prophets of Israel would say that another King would come through the line of David who would rule in Israel forever, and would make all things new again. The prophets told of one who would come and make a new covenant with Israel. He would give the people a new heart that desires to be obedient to God's Word and would be faithful to worship Him.

But not everything was perfect in Israel. The kings began to adopt the strategies and religious traditions of the people around them. They married the daughters of kings who worshiped idols and formed treaties with the nations. They stopped remembering the instructions they had been given at Sinai. They stopped remembering to keep the feasts and traditions that reminded them of who they were—God's special people—and over time they themselves fell into the worship of idols.

DAY 1: DAVID'S THRONE 95

Eventually, the once great nation was split into two—the northern kingdom of Israel, and the southern kingdom of Judah. Both kingdoms would ultimately be taken into captivity. But the prophets still told of a day when the Lord would restore Israel once again, a day when the Anointed One would come and the whole world would worship the one true God.

The people of Judah eventually did come back home, but their restoration didn't look anything like the prophets had talked about. They rebuilt the Temple, but it was nothing like the original one. In their hearts they knew that what the prophets had talked about had still not completely happened. The Anointed One had not yet come. So they lived in expectation of that day.

Searching the Scripture

Read 2 Samuel 7:8-11, 16:

> Now then, tell my servant David, "This is what the Lord Almighty says: I took you from the pasture, from tending the flock, and appointed you ruler over my people Israel. I have been with you wherever you have gone, and I have cut off all your enemies from before you. Now I will make your name great, like the names of the greatest men on

WEEK 4

earth. And I will provide a place for my people Israel and will plant them so that they can have a home of their own and no longer be disturbed. Wicked people will not oppress them anymore, as they did at the beginning and have done ever since the time I appointed leaders over my people Israel. I will also give you rest from all your enemies."

The Lord declares to you that the Lord himself will establish a house for you . . .

"Your house and your kingdom will endure forever before me; your throne will be established forever."

Answer the following questions:

- What did the Lord say He would do for David?

- What did the Lord say He would do for His special people, Israel?

DAY 1: DAVID'S THRONE   97

- Who will establish a house for David?

- How long will this house and kingdom endure?

Yielding to the Spirit

Know

We see in 1 Samuel that when the prophet came to David's father's home to anoint the next king over Israel, David's father, Jesse, didn't even bother to call David in from the field. He didn't have the kingly look that his brothers had. But Scripture tells us that it was God Himself who took David from the pasture and made him ruler over His special people. God is able to find people in places of obscurity and drop them in places of significance as He sees fit.

Now we see that not only did God make David a king, He also promised that his kingdom would never end.

98 WEEK 4

Later prophecies would clarify this even further—the Anointed One, the long-awaited Messiah, would actually be the fulfillment of this promise of God to David.

> "The days are coming," declares the Lord, "when I will raise up for David a righteous Branch, a King who will reign wisely and do what is just and right in the land. In his days Judah will be saved and Israel will live in safety. This is the name by which he will be called: The Lord Our Righteous Savior" (Jeremiah 23:5-6).

Be

God has a plan and a vision for your life just like David. At times you may feel that you have been overlooked (like David was by his father in the beginning). At times you may not feel qualified. But you are called and anointed for a purpose, and the things that God has promised you will surely come to pass if you will remain faithful to Him no matter what.

Do

What has God promised to you that has been delayed or even seems impossible? Write it down in the

DAY 1: DAVID'S THRONE 99

space here and recommit yourself in prayer to fully trust and obey the Lord in the process.

When you meet with your discipleship partner this week, share the promises that you have written down. Allow yourself to be vulnerable in talking about the things that you have been seeking from the Lord. After your discipleship partner has shared their writing, take some time to pray for one another with these hopes and dreams in focus. Continue to encourage one another in the days and weeks ahead as you share victories and challenges.

100 WEEK 4

Day 2

A New Start

Searching the Scripture

Read Isaiah 11:1-9:

> A shoot will come up from the stump of Jesse;
> from his roots a Branch will bear fruit. The
> Spirit of the Lord will rest on him—the Spirit
> of wisdom and of understanding, the Spirit of
> counsel and of might, the Spirit of the
> knowledge and fear of the Lord—and he will
> delight in the fear of the Lord. He will not
> judge by what he sees with his eyes, or decide
> by what he hears with his ears; but with right-
> eousness he will judge the needy, with justice
> he will give decisions for the poor of the earth.
> He will strike the earth with the rod of his
> mouth; with the breath of his lips he will slay
> the wicked. Righteousness will be his belt and
> faithfulness the sash around his waist. The
> wolf will live with the lamb, the leopard will lie
> down with the goat, the calf and the lion and
> the yearling together; and a little child will
> lead them. The cow will feed with the bear,
> their young will lie down together, and the lion
> will eat straw like the ox. The infant will play
> near the cobra's den, the young child will put
> its hand into the viper's nest. They will neither
> harm nor destroy on all my holy mountain, for

the earth will be filled with the knowledge of
the Lord as the waters cover the sea.

Answer the following questions:

- What will come up out of the stump of Jesse?

- Who will rest upon Him?

- What will He delight in?

- How will He judge and make decisions?

- How will He strike the earth and slay the wicked?

- What will be His belt and sash around His waist?

- With what will the whole earth be filled?

Yielding to the Spirit

Know

Even with the promising beginning of David's reign
as king, it only took one generation after him to introduce

DAY 2: A NEW START   103

idolatry back into Israel. Eventually, the nation split into two (Israel, the northern kingdom, and Judah, the southern kingdom). Idolatry and disobedience to God's law won the day in Israel and they were taken into captivity. When the small remnant of the once-great nation returned to Israel, it seemed that all was lost. This prophetic word was directed to them. The tree that represented the former glory of the kingdom of Israel had been cut down. Nothing was left but a stump. But that was all that God needed. God used their time in exile to correct them and remind them of who they were—His special people. He is the God who keeps His word, and out of this remnant, new hope was going to spring forth like a shoot emerging from a tree stump. All of creation would be blessed as a result.

Be

When God speaks a word of promise over our lives, He is faithful to do what He says He will do, if we will only be obedient and faithful to Him. Sometimes, in order to accomplish His purposes, some things have to be cut back in our lives. In John 15, Jesus compared it to a master gardener who prunes branches so that they will become fruitful. Those branches could represent unbiblical thinking and

104 WEEK 4

ungodly behavior patterns. They could be relationships that are toxic to our spiritual growth and maturity. Whatever they may be, at times it may seem as if God has allowed our whole world to crumble around us. But He doesn't need much to fulfill everything He said He would do. Like a small green shoot out of a tree stump, new life will suddenly break out in the middle of what seems like hopeless rubble.

What are some areas of your life that seem to have been cut down like the tree in this passage of Scripture that represented Israel's former glory? In other words, what circumstances in your life are making you believe there is no way that God's Word could possibly come to pass in your life. Take a moment to write these down in the space below.

Do

In the space below, jot down your thoughts about what God may be accomplishing in your life through the

DAY 2: A NEW START 105

circumstances you mentioned above. How might God work through your life in the days to come as a result of what He is doing right now? If you need to, talk about it with your discipleship partner and/or your pastor to get some outside perspective. In particular, be attentive to things in which God is calling you to obey His leading. What practical steps do you need to take to cooperate with God's restorative work? Prayerfully determine a practical step you need to take this week and commit to take it.

WEEK 4

Day 3

Small Things

Searching the Scripture

Read Micah 5:2-4:

> But you, Bethlehem Ephrathah, though you are small among the clans of Judah, out of you will come for me one who will be ruler over Israel, whose origins are from of old, from ancient times. Therefore Israel will be abandoned until the time when she who is in labor bears a son, and the rest of his brothers return to join the Israelites. He will stand and shepherd his flock in the strength of the Lord, in the majesty of the name of the Lord his God. And they will live securely, for then his greatness will reach to the ends of the earth.

Answer the following questions:

- What is significant about Bethlehem Ephrathah in this passage?

- Who will come out of Bethlehem?

WEEK 4

- When will Israel no longer be abandoned?

- What will the one spoken of do when He comes?

- How will His flock live?

Yielding to the Spirit

Know

This prophecy is directed to the city of Bethlehem, the city from which David's family came. In a way, by mentioning it the prophet is taking the people of Israel back to the beginning of God's promise to David. God is relentless about keeping His word. As you read yesterday, it seemed that all hope was lost in Israel, but God didn't need much to work with to save the world—just the stump of Jesse, a mere fragment of the former glory of Israel. In a similar way, this prophecy was not directed at a large city. The

DAY 3: SMALL THINGS 109

Messiah was not going to come out of the most populated city or the economic center of the nation of Israel. Instead, He was going to come from Bethlehem, a seemingly insignificant town at the time. But now it has become known as the place of the birth of Jesus Christ!

Be

God does not need our best efforts at kingdom building to bring about His plan to save all creation. Not only that, He purposely seems to choose small, seemingly unimportant things to work through. How will God bring about His plan and purpose for your life? It may begin with a small, apparently insignificant step. A seemingly unimportant person in your church may be the key person who will pray for you or speak a word into your life. It may come in the form of a minor task that seems like a distraction but is actually the beginning of a whole new calling and purpose.

Do

Ask the Holy Spirit to reveal the seemingly insignificant things in your life that you may have been avoiding or ignoring. Where have you allowed your priorities and

WEEK 4

ways of doing things to trump the Spirit's leading in your life? Ask the Lord to forgive you for not being carefully attentive to His leading, then seek Him for fresh direction. Jot down your impression of what the Holy Spirit may be saying to you in response to your prayer. Don't overlook instructions or opportunities that appear on the surface to be insignificant.

If you have any questions or are unsure about what the Lord might be saying to you, seek wisdom from trusted, spiritually mature Christians in your People of the Spirit group and in your local church.

Day 4

A New Heart

Searching the Scripture

Read Ezekiel 11:17-21:

> "Therefore say: 'This is what the Sovereign Lord says: I will gather you from the nations and bring you back from the countries where you have been scattered, and I will give you back the land of Israel again.'

> "They will return to it and remove all its vile images and detestable idols. I will give them an undivided heart and put a new spirit in them; I will remove from them their heart of stone and give them a heart of flesh. Then they will follow my decrees and be careful to keep my laws. They will be my people, and I will be their God. But as for those whose hearts are devoted to their vile images and detestable idols, I will bring down on their own heads what they have done, declares the Sovereign Lord."

Answer the following questions:

- What will the Lord's people do when they return to Israel?

112 WEEK 4

- What is the Lord going to give them?

- What is the Lord going to remove from them?

- What will the Lord's people do as a result?

- What will happen to those whose hearts are devoted to idols?

Yielding to the Spirit

Know

At the end of week 2, you read from Deuteronomy 30:15-20 where Moses prophesied to the Israelites that they had a choice. If they obeyed the commandments God had given them, they could dwell in the land He had promised to them. But if they were disobedient to Him, they would not be able to stay; God would scatter them abroad. The purpose of His discipline was to bring them back to Himself. Ezekiel's message to the people of God was about the faithfulness and holiness of God. Their kings and religious leaders had failed to lead them in following

DAY 4: A NEW HEART 113

the Lord. But the Lord had not forgotten them, and would one day restore them to the Promised Land under the leadership of a righteous ruler.[7]

Be

If you have been involved in church for any period of time, you have more than likely been challenged by the teachings of Jesus in the Sermon on the Mount or perhaps the Ten Commandments that we have already considered during the course of this study. There is a trap that is so easy to fall into when we begin to try to live our lives according to the teachings of Scripture. We fall into that trap when we attempt to live this way strictly out of our own efforts at self-discipline, trying to become a better person.

This ultimately leads to one of two major outcomes. The first is a sense of defeat and despair, when you finally realize you don't have what is needed to make the changes that need to be made. People have given up on following the Lord with all their hearts, sometimes completely walking away from the faith, resigned to their fate. Others

---

[7] Ralph H. Alexander, "Ezekiel," in *The Expositor's Bible Commentary: Jeremiah-Ezekiel*, ed. David E. Garland and Tremper Longman III (Grand Rapids, MI: Zondervan, 2010), p. 649.

114 WEEK 4

experience some surface-level success at changing their behavior, but are unaware of emotional issues and thought-processes that are just as bad as any behavior. Sometimes this group tends to become guilty of spiritual pride, comparing their spiritual maturity and strength to others who are weaker and less spiritual.

God had a plan to address this issue. The Scripture reading today speaks of a time, after the restoration of the people of God to the Promised Land, that the Lord would do something that had never been done before. Instead of simply giving them a written law, He would give them a new spirit. Instead of their stony, rebellious hearts, He was going to give them a tender heart (a heart of flesh) that would desire to follow Him. When they were restored, God was going to do something to change them from the inside out! We know now that this has been accomplished, first through the life, death, and resurrection of God's only Son, the promised Messiah, Jesus Christ (who we will discuss more in week 5). Second, it is being accomplished for all generations who will accept God's offer of salvation through Jesus through the ministry of the Holy Spirit (who will be discussed in week 6).

DAY 4: A NEW HEART 115

Do

Are there things in your life that you are struggling to overcome in your own strength? Perhaps it is a habit of some kind or an addictive behavior, or it may be related to your emotions (chronic depression, bad temper, etc.) that you can't seem to change no matter how hard you try. Write it down in the space below. As you do, reflect on your efforts. How much have you been trying to make changes in your own power (your intellectual ability, your self-discipline, your physical ability)? Have you truly gone before the Lord and asked Him to change your heart? His work can be a process; it may not happen overnight. Have you submitted yourself to His leading and His transforming grace? Take a moment to pray over these challenges you have written in this space and ask the Lord for His help and guidance to transform you from the inside out.

116 WEEK 4

Day 5

Comfort My People

Searching the Scripture

Read Isaiah 40:1-5:

> Comfort, comfort my people, says your God. Speak tenderly to Jerusalem, and proclaim to her that her hard service has been completed, that her sin has been paid for, that she has received from the Lord's hand double for all her sins. A voice of one calling: "In the wilderness prepare the way for the Lord; make straight in the desert a highway for our God. Every valley shall be raised up, every mountain and hill made low; the rough ground shall become level, the rugged places a plain. And the glory of the Lord will be revealed, and all people will see it together. For the mouth of the Lord has spoken."

Answer the following questions:

- What does God want to do for His people?

- How is God speaking to Jerusalem?

- What is God saying to Jerusalem?

WEEK 4

- What is the voice saying to do in the wilderness?

- What is going to be revealed?

- How will the people see it?

- Who has spoken that this is to be so?

Yielding to the Spirit

Know

Even with the promising beginning of David's reign as king, it took only one generation after him to introduce idolatry back into Israel. Eventually, the nation split into two (Israel, the northern kingdom, and Judah, the southern kingdom). Idolatry and disobedience to God's law won the day in Israel, and they were eventually taken into captivity. Later Judah, also guilty of idolatry and rebellion against God, went into captivity in Babylon. It is to this group that Isaiah writes these words. It is a reminder of the promise of the Messiah and the restoration of all things. It is a message of hope and comfort in a time of distress. It is also a

DAY 5: COMFORT MY PEOPLE   119

message of preparation. While they are still in their wilderness (that in-between time of God's promise and its fulfillment), they are called to prepare the way of the Lord.

Be

When we find ourselves waiting on the fulfillment of the promises of God, it can become difficult at times—especially when we are facing circumstances that seem totally opposite of what God has promised He would do. But the Lord is with us even in our times of trial. He has never abandoned us, and He is encouraging us to not give up on His promises. Just like the case of God's special people, even if we have caused a hindrance by our own sin, God can still restore. He will do what He said He would do. Write down some ways that God has encouraged you in times when you felt that His promises were being delayed in your life.

Do

As you reflect on the things that God has spoken to you, take a moment to write down ways that you can be

120 WEEK 4

preparing while you are in your wilderness. What are some steps of faith you need to take to be obedient to the leading of the Lord? What instructions do you feel the Lord has given you? Write them down here, then prayerfully develop a plan of action to accomplish at least one of them in an appropriate time frame. Share your thoughts with your discipleship partner this week and commit to continue praying for one another.

Week 5

Day 1

A New Day Dawns

Learning the Story

From the beginning, God promised that He had a plan to save us all. In the Garden of Eden, God Himself prophesied that the seed of the woman would crush the serpent's head (Genesis 3:15). He promised Abraham that He would see to it that Abraham's family would one day be a blessing to all the people groups of the world (Genesis 12:1-3). He had promised David that in his family line, the king's throne would be established forever (2 Samuel 7:16). And as we have already seen in week 4, the prophets continued to speak about the coming of the Messiah, the

122 WEEK 5

Anointed One who would restore Israel and establish God's kingdom in the Earth.

The last Old Testament prophet is actually written about in the New Testament. He is the one called John the Baptist. You can read about the story of John's parents, Zechariah and Elizabeth, and John's miraculous birth and ministry in the Gospel of Matthew (chapter 3), Mark (chapter 1), and Luke (chapters 1 and 3). He was the one whom the prophets said would come before the promised Messiah. His message was a simple one: Prepare for the coming of the Lord. His ministry was a call to repentance in anticipation of the coming of the long-awaited Messiah.

The day Israel had been looking to for so long finally came with the birth of Jesus, the Son of God. This is the high point of the story. Everything in the past pointed toward this moment and everything in the future looks back to it. Jesus was a faithful Jew who fulfilled all the words of the prophets, and He lived a life of faithfulness to God. What God had done in part through Moses, He would do completely through His Son, Jesus. Mankind was in slavery to sin and death. Jesus had come to lead them out in a new exodus. But the way He did it was unexpected. He gave His life on the cross to become the ultimate sacrifice for our

DAY 1: A NEW DAY DAWNS 123

sins even though He himself had never sinned. Three days after He died, He rose from the dead, and with His resurrection, a new day dawned. The new exodus had begun. What was lost in Eden in Genesis 3 would once again be restored to humanity.

Searching the Scripture

Read Luke 1:26-38:

> In the sixth month of Elizabeth's pregnancy, God sent the angel Gabriel to Nazareth, a town in Galilee, to a virgin pledged to be married to a man named Joseph, a descendant of David. The virgin's name was Mary. The angel went to her and said, "Greetings, you who are highly favored! The Lord is with you."
>
> Mary was greatly troubled at his words and wondered what kind of greeting this might be. But the angel said to her, "Do not be afraid, Mary; you have found favor with God. You will conceive and give birth to a son, and you are to call him Jesus. He will be great and will be called the Son of the Most High. The Lord God will give him the throne of his father David, and he will reign over Jacob's descendants forever; his kingdom will never end."
>
> "How will this be," Mary asked the angel, "since I am a virgin?"

124   WEEK 5

The angel answered, "The Holy Spirit will come on you, and the power of the Most High will overshadow you. So the holy one to be born will be called the Son of God. Even Elizabeth your relative is going to have a child in her old age, and she who was said to be unable to conceive is in her sixth month. For no word from God will ever fail."

"I am the Lord's servant," Mary answered. "May your word to me be fulfilled." Then the angel left her."

Answer the following questions:

- To whom did the angel come in this text?

- What did the angel say was going to happen to her?

- What was Mary going to call her Son?

- What else would He be called by others?

- What will the Lord God give to Him? What will He do as a result?

- How did the angel say this is going to happen to Mary?

DAY 1: A NEW DAY DAWNS   125

- As a result of the circumstances of His birth, what would He be called?

- What was Mary's response?

Yielding to the Spirit

Know

God was breaking into the middle of a world gone terribly wrong. Humanity was so far off course that there seemed to be no hope of return. By their decisions, God's people had positioned themselves as enemies of God. They had violated His law and worshiped idols. They had violated His very nature of love, righteousness, and justice. Almost from the beginning, humanity had attempted to choose its own path to fulfillment, apart from living life God's way. So, God, our heavenly Father, who had never stopped loving His good creation and had always been working to save us, decided it was now the right time to come on the scene Himself. And so Jesus entered into our world. In a way that is a mystery to us, God became a man and yet continued being God.

WEEK 5

He was going to come through this young virgin girl named Mary. Of course a natural question to ask was, *how are you going to do this*? Pay close attention to what the angel said to her: "the Holy Spirit will come upon you . . . the power of the Most High will overshadow you." This was not some kind of veiled reference to a god having sexual relations with a human being. This was a creative act of the Holy Spirit, and it should sound familiar. It is just like what happened in Genesis 1 when the Spirit hovered over the dark, watery void.

This was the beginning of the story of the man Jesus. But it was also the new beginning of the human story. Once again, the Holy Spirit was hovering over the chaos of creation. Once again, He was bringing order out of disorder. He was going to bring purpose out of chaos. What was forfeited was going to be redeemed. Through Jesus, everything was going to be given back to the Father. And it all began here. The disorder of this world was going to be set right by Jesus Christ, the head of a new race of humanity who would one day rule the redeemed and restored world on God's behalf.

DAY 1: A NEW DAY DAWNS 127

Be

At the very beginning of this study, in the first group encounter, the topic was on creation in Genesis 1. The Holy Spirit hovered over the creation that was in chaos because God was about to do something new. Now we see the same thing happening again; this time, however, in the life of a young, virgin girl. Her response to the angel's message is challenging to us, "May your word to me be fulfilled." She was willing for God to do whatever He desired to do in and through her. It is a model for how each of us should respond to the work of the Lord in our lives.

Do

By this time, if you have been faithfully working through these readings, you have had ample opportunity to reflect on what the Holy Spirit is saying to you. Perhaps you have become aware of some things about your personal life that God is working to effect change—in your thoughts, your emotions, your will, and/or your physical body. Make a short list of things that you sense the Lord wanting to address, and beside each item write what your response has been thus far. Where do you see resistance? What do you think is causing it? In your prayer time, give

128 WEEK 5

those things to the Lord and ask Him to help you come to a place of surrender to Him. Are there ways that you can lean upon your discipleship partner for support, encouragement, and accountability to make real progress in these areas?

Day 2

Jesus' Baptism and Temptation

Searching the Scripture

Read Luke 3:21-22:

> When all the people were being baptized, Jesus was baptized too. And as he was praying, heaven was opened and the Holy Spirit descended on him in bodily form like a dove. And a voice came from heaven: "You are my Son, whom I love; with you I am well pleased."

Read Luke 4:1-2:

> Jesus, full of the Holy Spirit, left the Jordan and was led by the Spirit into the wilderness, where for forty days he was tempted by the devil. He ate nothing during those days, and at the end of them he was hungry.

130 WEEK 5

Answer the following questions:

- What happened to Jesus when He came to the place where John was baptizing the people?

- What happened to Jesus as He was praying?

- What did the voice from heaven say about Jesus?

- How does Luke describe Jesus as He was leaving the Jordan River?

- Where did the Spirit lead Jesus?

- What happened to Him there?

- How does Luke describe Jesus' condition at the end of 40 days of eating nothing?

DAY 2: JESUS' BAPTISM AND TEMPTATION

Yielding to the Spirit

Know

There is much to see in this portion of the Gospels that describe Jesus' life and ministry. We see here that Jesus fully identified with the human race in water baptism, although He had no sin for which He should repent. At the same time, the witness of His true identity was testified to by the Holy Spirit's descent on Him in the form of a dove and the voice of the Father out of Heaven declaring Jesus to be His beloved Son. Almost from the beginning, theologians in the church have pointed to this event as a picture of the Trinity—Father, Son, and Holy Spirit. It is a mystery we cannot completely fathom, but God is three and God is one. And yet, at the same time, Jesus was both fully God and fully human. This is called the Incarnation. God became flesh and lived with us. In doing so, the distance that had once existed between humanity and God because of sin was overcome.

This divine/human nature of Jesus is a mystery. However, we are not left in doubt about the true humanity of Jesus. Immediately after His baptism, He was led by the Spirit of God into the wilderness to undergo temptation.

WEEK 5

After fasting for 40 days, Jesus was hungry. The enemy's temptation of Him was real. And, we find from reading the full account that Jesus' victory over the devil was just as real, and it shows us the way to do the same.

Be

Part of the power of reading the Gospels is to learn from Jesus how we are to live this life of being led by the Spirit in full cooperation with the will of the Father. All who believe and obey the gospel of Jesus Christ are declared by the Father to be beloved sons and daughters. And, like Jesus, the devil will immediately work to attack that identity. He will find you in moments of vulnerability—opportune times, as Luke calls it (4:13).

How has your identity as a beloved son or daughter of God been tested? What lies or deceptions has the enemy used against you to discourage you from the path of full obedience to the Father? Write your thoughts in this space.

DAY 2: JESUS' BAPTISM AND TEMPTATION

Do

A key step in the process of our spiritual growth is to choose to believe what God has said about you, no matter what circumstances say or how the devil is attempting to deceive. Talk with your discipleship peer about your areas of struggle with your identity as a beloved son or daughter of God. Help one another to replace lies of the devil with the truth of the Father as revealed in Scripture. Pray for one another to stand firm in the calling and identity given to each of you by our loving Father God. Seek ways to help others do the same.

134 WEEK 5

Day 3

Jesus' Death

Searching the Scripture

Read Luke 22:33-46:

> When they came to the place called the Skull, they crucified him there, along with the criminals—one on his right, the other on his left. Jesus said, "Father, forgive them, for they do not know what they are doing." And they divided up his clothes by casting lots.
>
> The people stood watching, and the rulers even sneered at him. They said, "He saved others; let him save himself if he is God's Messiah, the Chosen One."
>
> The soldiers also came up and mocked him. They offered him wine vinegar and said, "If you are the king of the Jews, save yourself."
>
> There was a written notice above him, which read: THIS IS THE KING OF THE JEWS.
>
> One of the criminals who hung there hurled insults at him: "Aren't you the Messiah? Save yourself and us!"

136 WEEK 5

But the other criminal rebuked him. "Don't you fear God," he said, "since you are under the same sentence? We are punished justly, for we are getting what our deeds deserve. But this man has done nothing wrong."

Then he said, "Jesus, remember me when you come into your kingdom."

Jesus answered him, "Truly I tell you, today you will be with me in paradise."

It was now about noon, and darkness came over the whole land until three in the afternoon, for the sun stopped shining. And the curtain of the temple was torn in two. Jesus called out with a loud voice, "Father, into your hands I commit my spirit." When he had said this, he breathed his last."

Answer the following questions:

- With whom was Jesus crucified?

- As He was being crucified, what did Jesus say to the Father (first quote of two)?

- What was written above Jesus on the cross?

- What did one of the criminals say to insult Jesus?

DAY 3: JESUS' DEATH 137

- What did the other criminal say to Jesus?

- What were Jesus' final words just before He died?

Yielding to the Spirit

Know

In Jesus, God and humanity came together. But the problem of sin still remained. The effects of Adam and Eve's decision to rebel in the Garden of Eden (Genesis 3) were still present. The end result of their actions was death—spiritual and physical. God had implemented a system of sacrifices for His people to use as they approached Him in their sinful condition. But, as one writer in Scripture said,

> It is impossible for the blood of bulls and goats to take away sins. Therefore, when Christ came into the world, he said: "Sacrifice and offering you did not desire, but a body you prepared for me; with burnt offerings and sin offerings you were not pleased. Then I said, 'Here I am—it is written about me in the scroll—I have come to do your will, my God'" (Hebrews 10:4-7).

138 WEEK 5

We will look at the full mission of Jesus in the Group Encounter at the end of this week. But at this point, it is important to understand that, in giving His life on the cross, Jesus paid the full price for the sin of humanity. In His death, He made forgiveness possible for all who will believe and obey the gospel.

Be

Our study is at the climax of the story of God. This part of God's plan can never be overlooked or minimized. Without Jesus laying down His life for us, nothing else is possible. Are you truly grateful to Him for His willingness to sacrifice His life in this way? Are you truly grateful for the suffering He endured on our behalf? True gratitude will result in a willingness to lay down your own life for Him. For some, this has meant physical martyrdom in environments that are hostile to the faith. But for the majority of Christians, this is a willingness to surrender our ambitions, time, energy, and money to do our part to participate in God's plan to save the world. Jesus said, "Whoever wants to be my disciple must deny themselves and take up their cross daily and follow me" (Luke 9:23). Only in this way will we truly realize who we were meant to be.

DAY 3: JESUS' DEATH   139

Do

In your prayer time today allow the Holy Spirit to speak to you about the cross. Reflect on the cost that was paid to make our forgiveness possible. Then spend focused time offering thanks to the Lord for His faithfulness to the Father's will. Allow the Lord to speak to you about what it looks like for you to take up your cross as well. How can you give yourself obediently to God's mission to save His creation? Write your thoughts in this space.

140 WEEK 5

Day 4

Jesus' Resurrection

Searching the Scripture

Read Luke 24:36-49:

> While they were still talking about this, Jesus himself stood among them and said to them, "Peace be with you."

> They were startled and frightened, thinking they saw a ghost. He said to them, "Why are you troubled, and why do doubts rise in your minds? Look at my hands and my feet. It is I myself! Touch me and see; a ghost does not have flesh and bones, as you see I have."

> When he had said this, he showed them his hands and feet. And while they still did not believe it because of joy and amazement, he asked them, "Do you have anything here to eat?" They gave him a piece of broiled fish, and he took it and ate it in their presence.

> He said to them, "This is what I told you while I was still with you: Everything must be fulfilled that is written about me in the Law of Moses, the Prophets and the Psalms."

WEEK 5

Then he opened their minds so they could understand the Scriptures. He told them, "This is what is written: The Messiah will suffer and rise from the dead on the third day, and repentance for the forgiveness of sins will be preached in his name to all nations, beginning at Jerusalem. You are witnesses of these things. I am going to send you what my Father has promised; but stay in the city until you have been clothed with power from on high."

Answer the following questions:

- How did the disciples first react to Jesus' appearing among them?

- What did Jesus tell them to do when He saw they were afraid?

- When the disciples still didn't believe because of joy and amazement, what did Jesus do next?

- What did Jesus say had to be fulfilled?

- What did He say the disciples were witnesses of?

DAY 4: JESUS' RESURRECTION 143

- What is Jesus going to do next with the disciples?

Yielding to the Spirit

Know

Sin wasn't the only consequence of the Adam's disobedience in Eden. Death was the ultimate outcome. In Jesus, sin has been dealt with on the cross, but death has been dealt a fatal blow in the resurrection. We are now beginning to see God's true intention. He was not just making forgiveness possible for us; He was also doing something new. Jesus did not come back as a ghost. Ghosts don't eat! He came back in a physical body, but this body would never again experience sickness and death. Here we see a glimpse of the ultimate destiny for all who will be saved by faithful obedience to Him.

Resurrection is a centerpiece of the Christian faith. Other religions have a founding figure who died, but each is still dead. Jesus is the only one who died and came back to life with a transformed, spiritual body.

144   WEEK 5

Be

What are the implications of the resurrection for how we are to live right now? On the simplest level, we can say this—resurrection means that nothing is impossible with God. But certainly there is more. Paul said that in order to become part of God's people—God's family—two basic things are necessary, "If you declare with your mouth, 'Jesus is Lord,' and believe in your heart that God raised him from the dead, you will be saved" (Romans 10:9). Declare and believe. This is more than saying words or agreeing to something. It is basing our entire lives—every decision—on these two facts: Jesus is Lord and God raised Him from the dead. We are no longer our own god, doing what we see fit to do. That was the mistake Adam and Eve made in the garden. Now we acknowledge with our lives that Jesus is Lord. And, in some way that we may not completely understand, we can know that our lives will carry over into the life to come when we too will be given resurrection bodies to live with Him forever. These truths should inform our way of living every day.

DAY 4: JESUS' RESURRECTION

Do

What would it look like for you to fully live your life based on the confession, "Jesus is Lord, and God raised Him from the dead?" Have you fully submitted to His leadership in your life? Or do you just *say* that He is Lord? Have you limited what He can do in and through you? Or do you believe, based on the resurrection, that with God anything is possible? Write your reflections in the space below, then take them to the Lord. Confess to Him where you have not acknowledged the lordship of Jesus and where you have limited God's activity in your life. Finally, make the commitment, including practical steps in changing your behavior, to turn away from living that way and to turn toward living life in light of the truth revealed in today's reading.

146 WEEK 5

Day 5

Jesus' Ascension

Searching the Scripture

Read Mark 16:15-20:

> He said to them, "Go into all the world and preach the gospel to all creation. Whoever believes and is baptized will be saved, but whoever does not believe will be condemned. And these signs will accompany those who believe: In my name they will drive out demons; they will speak in new tongues; they will pick up snakes with their hands; and when they drink deadly poison, it will not hurt them at all; they will place their hands on sick people, and they will get well."
>
> After the Lord Jesus had spoken to them, he was taken up into heaven and he sat at the right hand of God. Then the disciples went out and preached everywhere, and the Lord worked with them and confirmed his word by the signs that accompanied it.

Answer the following questions:

- What did Jesus tell the disciples to do?

148 WEEK 5

- Who will be saved? Who will be condemned?

- What signs will accompany those who believe?

- In whose name will the signs take place?

- What happened to Jesus after He had spoken to them?

- What did the disciples do afterward?

- How was the Lord involved with the work of the disciples?

Yielding to the Spirit

Know

In the beginning, Adam and Eve walked with God in unbroken fellowship. Sin changed all of that. Because of their rebellion, the entire human race has had to endure the curse that fell on creation. Eden was lost, as was our fellowship with God. But from the beginning, God moved

DAY 5: JESUS' ASCENSION   149

toward us to restore all that had been lost. His plan took thousands of years to accomplish. From Adam, to Noah, to Abraham, to David, and ultimately to Jesus by way of the Virgin Birth, God's plan to save us all finally was fulfilled.

In Jesus' crucifixion, our sins are dealt with and forgiveness is made possible. In Jesus' resurrection, death is defeated, and we are given the promise of new life. As we will see next week, it is a promise we experience in part now, but will one day experience in its fullness. But, what is important about the ascension that is recorded in this passage? So often we overlook its significance.

Daniela Augustine, a professor at Lee University, wrote these words about the ascension of Jesus:

> Finally, in His ascension, Christ unites heaven and earth as their ultimate destiny in and with God, bringing humanity within the *koinonia* of the Trinity, making us "partakers of the divine nature" (2 Peter 1:4) and making possible our transfiguring into its likeness.[8]

Be

So then, what does the ascension mean for us? It means that in our representative, Jesus Christ, heaven and

---

[8] Daniela C. Augustine, *Pentecost, Hospitality, and Transfiguration: Toward a Spirit-Inspired Vision of Social Transformation* (Cleveland, TN: CPT Press, 2012), p. 22.

150 WEEK 5

earth have come together. The Scripture tells us that He is seated at the right hand of the Father (Mark 16:19), which is a place of authority. Furthermore, Paul said we are seated with Him in the heavenly realms (Ephesians 2:6). This means that, even now, God is giving to His people a share in Jesus' authority to enable us to accomplish the work that He has called us to do with Him.

Finally, according to 2 Peter 1:4, we participate in the divine nature. This means that, although we never become God (or even part of God), we become more and more like Him as the Holy Spirit lives in us and as we develop our relationship with Him through prayer, the reading of His Word, and participation in His family—the Church.

Do

If by this point you have not made the decision to accept Jesus as the Lord and Savior He is, then take a moment to reflect on what might be hindering you from that decision. What do you need to know? What do you need to hear? What is stopping you from fully believing that God can make all things new for you? Take your thoughts and concerns to a pastor or other mature Christian in your

DAY 5: JESUS' ASCENSION 151

church or People of the Spirit group and work with them as you make a decision to follow Jesus with your whole heart.

WEEK 5

Week 6

Day 1

Ascension and Commission

Learning the Story

In Jesus, we have finally reached the climax of the story. We saw the good beginning in the Garden of Eden, and we saw Eden lost because of sin and rebellion against God. We have seen the plan of God to restore and renew all things, beginning with the call of Abraham and the promise that his family for generations to come would be God's special people. We saw that family in slavery in Egypt and delivered under the anointed leadership of Moses.

We have read about the kind of people that God wanted Israel to be as we stood at the foot of Mount Sinai and heard the Ten Commandments. We have experienced

WEEK 6

the fearfulness of the people as they saw and heard the thunder and lightning, causing them to choose to distance themselves from God and allow Moses to be their mediator. We also realized how quickly God's people can start worshiping idols when they don't know or understand what God is doing. From the promise of a never-ending kingdom to David to the message of the prophets, there was one overriding message repeatedly given—the Messiah is coming to establish God's kingdom forever. He is the Seed of the woman, the Fulfillment of Abraham's promise, the Mediator sought by Israel, and the King whose kingdom would know no end.

Now He had come. And with Him came the message that the kingdom of God was near (Luke 10:9). But He came in a way the people didn't expect—a baby in a manger visited by shepherds, a child visited by kings from a faraway land bringing Him gifts. He was the Rabbi who surrounded Himself with fishermen, a tax collector, and a political activist (Simon the Zealot). And instead of establishing a visible kingdom, He suffered and died. But in His resurrection and ascension, a new day dawned.

The kingdom of God is here now, but not yet. The Lord will return one day to finish what has been started. In

DAY 1: ASCENSION AND COMMISSION 155

the meantime, there is still more to be done. People need to be told what has happened. They need to be invited to join God's family, to know His love, and to become part of His kingdom. Jesus has ascended, so who will do what is necessary?

Searching the Scripture

Read Acts 1:1-11:

> In my former book, Theophilus, I wrote about all that Jesus began to do and to teach until the day he was taken up to heaven, after giving instructions through the Holy Spirit to the apostles he had chosen. After his suffering, he presented himself to them and gave many convincing proofs that he was alive. He appeared to them over a period of forty days and spoke about the kingdom of God. On one occasion, while he was eating with them, he gave them this command: "Do not leave Jerusalem, but wait for the gift my Father promised, which you have heard me speak about. For John baptized with water, but in a few days you will be baptized with the Holy Spirit."
>
> Then they gathered around him and asked him, "Lord, are you at this time going to restore the kingdom to Israel?"
>
> He said to them: "It is not for you to know the times or dates the Father has set by his own authority. But you will receive power when the

156 WEEK 6

Holy Spirit comes on you; and you will be my witnesses in Jerusalem, and in all Judea and Samaria, and to the ends of the earth."

After he said this, he was taken up before their very eyes, and a cloud hid him from their sight.

They were looking intently up into the sky as he was going, when suddenly two men dressed in white stood beside them. "Men of Galilee," they said, "why do you stand here looking into the sky? This same Jesus, who has been taken from you into heaven, will come back in the same way you have seen him go into heaven."

Answer the following questions:

- What did Jesus do after His suffering?

- What did He speak about over a period of 40 days after His resurrection?

- For what did He tell the disciples to wait in Jerusalem?

- What did the disciples ask Jesus as they gathered around Him?

DAY 1: ASCENSION AND COMMISSION — 157

- Instead of telling them the answer they sought, what did Jesus tell them they would do?

- What happened after He told them they would be His witnesses to the ends of the earth?

Yielding to the Spirit

Know

It is important that we realize what Jesus left behind Him when He ascended. He left a group of people. And He left them with an instruction: Don't leave Jerusalem until you receive the promise you heard me speak about (Acts 1:4).

They gathered around Him and asked Him, "Lord, are you at this time going to restore the kingdom to Israel?" (Acts 1:6). They still didn't quite understand God's plan, but that would change soon. In the meantime, all they needed to know was that they were going to receive power from Him to become His witnesses. We are called to be filled with His Spirit and to be fruitful, multiply, and fill the earth with men, women, boys, and girls, who acknowledge

WEEK 6

Him as King and Savior. We have authority over Satan and his kingdom of darkness as we work hand-in-hand with the Holy Spirit to advance the Kingdom. One day, Jesus himself will return to the earth to finish what He started and bring all of creation together in Him. In that day, every eye will see Him and everyone will know that He is King of all kings.

Be

In this passage, the disciples were focused on an earthly kingdom. It was their best understanding of what they thought God had promised to do. But God's plan is bigger than an earthly kingdom. What He is doing is for all nations and all generations. Ultimately, He doesn't intend to establish His kingdom in the earth as it is today. He is going to make all things new. Eden will be restored. The disciples (nor us, for that matter) could not really get their minds around the scope of God's plan.

As we live our lives, it is so easy to get caught up in our own agenda. Like the disciples we tend to ask the Lord, "*Now* are you going to make this happen for me?" "*Now* are you going to give me this opportunity?" "*Now* are you going to solve my problem?" But we have to keep in mind

DAY 1: ASCENSION AND COMMISSION

the bigger picture of what God is doing. Furthermore, we have to keep in mind that our purpose is wrapped up in God's plans. He cares about our lives, and He takes an interest in the smallest of things. Out of that loving relationship with Him, we are called to be His witnesses. We can never get sidetracked from that mission.

What things are you focusing on that may be taking your attention away from the mission God has called you to be part of? Write them here.

Do

In your prayer time today, ask the Lord to renew your focus on His mission. Talk with Him specifically about things that are a worry and distraction to you. Give your concerns and cares to Him and rest in His love for you. Then ask the Lord to show you how you can be more involved with His mission to spread the good news of what has been accomplished in Jesus. Begin today walking in obedience to His leadership.

160 WEEK 6

Day 2

Pentecost

Searching the Scripture

Read Acts 2:1-4; 14-2:1:

> When the day of Pentecost came, they were all together in one place. Suddenly a sound like the blowing of a violent wind came from heaven and filled the whole house where they were sitting. They saw what seemed to be tongues of fire that separated and came to rest on each of them. All of them were filled with the Holy Spirit and began to speak in other tongues as the Spirit enabled them.
>
> Then Peter stood up with the Eleven, raised his voice and addressed the crowd: "Fellow Jews and all of you who live in Jerusalem, let me explain this to you; listen carefully to what I say. These people are not drunk, as you suppose. It's only nine in the morning! No, this is what was spoken by the prophet Joel:
>
> 'In the last days, God says, I will pour out my Spirit on all people. Your sons and daughters will prophesy, your young men will see visions, your old men will dream dreams. Even

162 WEEK 6

on my servants, both men and women, I will pour out my Spirit in those days, and they will prophesy. I will show wonders in the heavens above and signs on the earth below, blood and fire and billows of smoke. The sun will be turned to darkness and the moon to blood before the coming of the great and glorious day of the Lord. And everyone who calls on the name of the Lord will be saved.'

Answer the following questions:

- Where were the disciples when the Day of Pentecost came?

- What did they hear?

- What did they see?

- What did they do when they were filled with the Holy Spirit?

- What prophet did Peter say had spoken of this event?

- What did the prophet say God would do?

DAY 2: PENTECOST 163

- Who will the Lord pour out His Spirit upon in the last days?

- Who will be saved?

Yielding to the Spirit

Know

Not only was Joel's prophecy fulfilled, but Jesus' own words to His disciples spoken just before His ascension were as well. He had promised to send them the Holy Spirit, and from that experience, He would launch them out into a ministry that would ultimately go around the world!

As Pentecostal people, we believe that we are continuing to live out the story told in the Book of Acts. Just as the Holy Spirit fell on the Day of Pentecost in the Upper Room, He continues to be poured out today. We believe in the fivefold gospel—Jesus is Savior, Sanctifier, Spirit-baptizer, Healer, and soon-coming King. Just as Jesus poured out His Spirit on that day, He continues to do so to this very day. Millions around the world have had the experience of the baptism in the Holy Spirit accompanied

164 WEEK 6

by the manifestation of speaking in tongues. Have you had this experience?

Be

Just before the ascension, Jesus placed great importance on this encounter with His disciples. He insisted they wait on the outpouring of the Spirit before they attempted to engage in the mission of God. Even Jesus' own mother needed this experience, which should give us something to think about.

God's people should have a desire for spiritual fullness. It should be normal for us to accept everything that the Lord is offering to us as He sends us out into the sometimes hostile world to be His witnesses. We don't know everything we need to know to do God's work, but the Holy Spirit—who is God—does know. We need His presence and power in our lives. What are some things that might be hindering you from receiving the baptism in the Holy Spirit? Write them here and be prepared to talk to the Lord about them in your prayer time.

DAY 2: PENTECOST

Do

If you have never experienced the baptism in the Holy Spirit begin to pray about it during your prayer time. Be honest with the Lord about any misgivings or concerns you may have, but be open to what He desires to do in your life. Some things can be understood only when they are experienced! You may also want to talk with your pastor or another trusted leader in your local church to help answer any questions you may have and to have someone to pray with and for you as you seek all God has for you.

If you have experienced the baptism in the Holy Spirit, how has that experience empowered you for more effective involvement in the mission of God? Remember that was the purpose in Acts—to launch the Church into global ministry. What part are you called to play in that mission? What steps do you need to take today to position yourself for obedience to your calling?

166 WEEK 6

Day 3

Persecution and Expansion

Searching the Scripture

Read Acts 8:1-4:

> And Saul approved of their killing him [Stephen]. On that day a great persecution broke out against the church in Jerusalem, and all except the apostles were scattered throughout Judea and Samaria. Godly men buried Stephen and mourned deeply for him. But Saul began to destroy the church. Going from house to house, he dragged off both men and women and put them in prison. Those who had been scattered preached the word wherever they went.

Answer the following questions:

- Who approved of the killing of Stephen?

- What broke out against the church on that day?

WEEK 6

- Where were the Christians (except the apostles) scattered?

- What did Saul begin doing?

- What did those who had been scattered do?

Yielding to the Spirit

Know

This is an account of the first martyr of the church, named Stephen. A martyr is one who dies because of His faithfulness to the Lord. Not only did Stephen die, but also out of this event there arose a wave of persecution led by a man named Saul. We will revisit Saul in tomorrow's reading. But for now, notice what happened to the Church during this time—they were scattered. The Christians fled Jerusalem and went to Judea and Samaria. Now let's go back and see what Jesus told the disciples just before He ascended:

> But you will receive power when the Holy
> Spirit comes on you; and you will be my wit-

DAY 3: PERSECUTION AND EXPANSION 169

nesses in Jerusalem, and in all Judea and Samaria, and to the ends of the earth (Acts 1:8).

Do you see the connection? The gospel did indeed
leave Jerusalem and go to Judea and Samaria, and ultimately it will go the ends of the earth. But the way that it happened is probably not the way that anyone expected, nor is
it likely that anyone would have chosen it. People normally
don't pray for persecution and hardship. But because we
have an enemy, it is part of the Christian story and will
continue to be so until the Lord returns to make all things
new. Until then, God has a way of turning bad things into
good things. Rather than stopping this little movement, the
persecution fanned the flame and the good news spread
even further than before.

Be

Perhaps you have surrendered your life to the Lord
and have experienced the presence and power of the Holy
Spirit in your life. That doesn't mean you won't face struggles and even suffering at times. We live in a world that is
still subject to the curse that fell on it in the Garden of
Eden. We have an enemy that has been trying to interfere
with God's plan since then as well. You and I are no excep-

tion. But you must always keep in mind that what Satan intends to harm you, God will use for good (Genesis 50:20). Your future, your needs, your very identity is secure in the Lord's hands. Don't be discouraged when things get tough. "Consider it pure joy, my brothers and sisters, whenever you face trials of many kinds, because you know that the testing of your faith produces perseverance" (James 1:2–3).

Do

How is your faithful obedience to the Lord being hindered right now? Are there circumstances related to life in general that are causing you concern? Are you experiencing a spiritual struggle? Are you facing sickness in your physical body? When you meet with your discipleship peer this week, share as much as you feel comfortable sharing with him/her and ask your peer to pray with you about it. Then allow your peer to do the same. Remember that Scripture teaches us, "Carry each other's burdens, and in this way you will fulfill the law of Christ" (Galatians 6:2). Be faithful to continue being obedient to God's call on your life. Trust the Lord to redeem any negative situations for your good and for the good of His mission.

Day 4

One New Humanity

Searching the Scripture

Read Ephesians 2:11-18:

> Therefore, remember that formerly you who are Gentiles by birth and called "uncircumcised" by those who call themselves "the circumcision" (which is done in the body by human hands)—remember that at that time you were separate from Christ, excluded from citizenship in Israel and foreigners to the covenants of the promise, without hope and without God in the world. But now in Christ Jesus you who once were far away have been brought near by the blood of Christ.
>
> For he himself is our peace, who has made the two groups one and has destroyed the barrier, the dividing wall of hostility, by setting aside in his flesh the law with its commands and regulations. His purpose was to create in himself one new humanity out of the two, thus making peace, and in one body to reconcile both of them to God through the cross, by which he put to death their hostility. He came and preached peace to you who were far away and peace to those who were near. For

172 WEEK 6

through him we both have access to the Father by one Spirit.

Answer the following questions:

- What were these Gentiles formerly called?

- Who called them that?

- What was the Gentiles' status with regard to Christ at the time those things were being said?

- What was their relationship to Israel?

- How were those who were far away from God brought near to Him?

- What did Jesus do with the two groups (Jews and Gentiles)?

DAY 4: ONE NEW HUMANITY 173

- What was His purpose in doing this?

- How did He do this?

- Through Christ we have access to whom? By whom?

Yielding to the Spirit

Know

It should be interesting to you to know who wrote these words. Do you remember Saul who was responsible for leading the first major wave of persecution against the Church? He wrote these words! (You can read about his conversion to Christianity in Acts 9.) But *what* is written here is even more important than *who* wrote these words.

Biblically speaking, you could say that there really were only two major groups of people during the time of Christ—Jews (descendants of Abraham and those who had converted to Judaism) and Gentiles (everyone else). The church started out as a sect made up of Jewish believers. But it quickly became apparent that God was not done. We get the first hint that God is about to open the door even wider when we read what happened to Peter in Acts 10. To get right to the point, God gave Peter a vision, Peter went and preached to a group of Gentiles, and the Holy Spirit fell on them just like He had on the Jews on the Day of Pentecost!

This presented quite the challenge to the Jewish believers as to what to do next. Should they require them to completely obey the law God had given Moses at Sinai? Or was God not requiring that any longer? Over time, they worked out those issues, but it took effort and a commitment to be faithful to the full meaning of what had been accomplished through Jesus.

Be

Just as the Jewish believers struggled with accepting the Gentiles, we still have struggles in the church today. We find many ways to divide ourselves. Some of those ways include racial differences, worship styles, denominations, doctrines, and other various preferences we often take far too seriously. There can be no denying

DAY 4: ONE NEW HUMANITY · 175

that many of these things create challenges for us. We may not completely agree on everything, and we certainly can't change who we are, ethnically speaking. But we must keep this in mind—the gospel of Christ is a gospel that brings together people from all walks of life. When we surrender our lives to Him, we become part of His family. His family is quite diverse! The key is that we all keep our eyes on Jesus and seek to live, love, and serve in the way that He has taught us. Since we are all seated with Him in heavenly places we need to figure out how to work together in unity. But always remember that unity does not require uniformity.

Do

Take an opportunity to get to know someone who is outside your normal comfort zone. Go to get coffee with them and visit. Ask questions and listen to them. Ask the Lord to help you enter into their world so you can see things from their perspective. You might be surprised what you learn!

In your prayer time today, ask the Lord to reveal any prejudice in your heart against any groups of people. Allow the Holy Spirit to show you where you have an us-

WEEK 6

and-them attitude toward others, particularly those who are part of the family of God. Repent for your attitude and ask the Lord to reveal His love for all people through you.

Day 5

Eden Restored

Searching the Scripture

Read Revelation 21:1-5; 22:1-7:

> Then I saw a new heaven and a new earth, for the first heaven and the first earth had passed away, and there was no longer any sea. I saw the Holy City, the new Jerusalem, coming down out of heaven from God, prepared as a bride beautifully dressed for her husband. And I heard a loud voice from the throne saying, "Look! God's dwelling place is now among the people, and he will dwell with them. They will be his people, and God himself will be with them and be their God. He will wipe every tear from their eyes. There will be no more death or mourning or crying or pain, for the old order of things has passed away." He who was seated on the throne said, "I am making everything new!" Then he said, "Write this down, for these words are trustworthy and true."

> Then the angel showed me the river of the water of life, as clear as crystal, flowing from the throne of God and of the Lamb down the middle of the great street of the city. On each side of the river stood the tree

WEEK 6

of life, bearing twelve crops of fruit, yielding its fruit every month. And the leaves of the tree are for the healing of the nations. No longer will there be any curse. The throne of God and of the Lamb will be in the city, and his servants will serve him. They will see his face, and his name will be on their foreheads. There will be no more night. They will not need the light of a lamp or the light of the sun, for the Lord God will give them light. And they will reign forever and ever.

The angel said to me, "These words are trustworthy and true. The Lord, the God who inspires the prophets, sent his angel to show his servants the things that must soon take place."

"Look, I am coming soon! Blessed is the one who keeps the words of the prophecy written in this scroll."

Answer the following questions:

- When John saw the new heaven and new earth what had happened to the first heaven and first earth?

- Where will God's dwelling place be?

DAY 5: EDEN RESTORED 179

- What happened to the old order of things?

- What did He who was seated on the throne say?

- What was on each side of the river flowing from the throne of God?

- What was the purpose of the leaves of the trees?

- What had become of the curse?

- Where will the throne of God and the Lamb be located?

- When is the Lord coming back?

Yielding to the Spirit

Know

Everything that went wrong in the Garden of Eden is going to be made right. This world fell victim to a catastrophe of cosmic proportions. That catastrophe was

WEEK 6

caused by the actions of Adam and Eve, making the decision to make their own rules instead of submitting to God's. One act of disobedience brought a curse on what was once a good creation. The authority that Adam and Eve, and all of their descendants, including us, were to have was handed over in one moment to the devil. The devil doesn't create; he destroys. He doesn't speak the truth; he traffics in lies. He is not the life-giver; he is the bringer of death. All disease, all chaos, all confusion, all hurt, all sorrow, all loss are to be attributed to the effects of his activity. And we gave him permission to do it.

Before the fall in the garden, humans were in a right relationship with God. Now we have grown so far from Him that we have created our own gods. Once we were in right relationship with one another, but now we manipulate, use, and even buy and sell one another like commodities so that we can have the things that we want. We use the devil's tactics of lying, destroying, and killing so that we can have power and control of our own little kingdoms.

But God broke into our world just like He said he would on that fateful day in the garden. He started with Abraham and promised that through him all the families of the earth would be blessed. And in the fullness of time, that

DAY 5: EDEN RESTORED   181

blessing came in the form of Jesus. He was crowned king with a crown of thorns and gave His life for all humanity. His resurrection was the dawn of the new creation. His ascension was His enthronement as king and brought us with Him into the presence of the Lord to share in His authority and power. One day He will return to make His kingdom complete. On that day, every knee will bow and every tongue will confess that He is Lord. On that day, everything that went wrong will be made right. On that day, the human race will be in right relationship with God, with each other, and with all of creation. On that day, God's goal of dwelling with us will be realized. And everything that we are hoping for will finally be made a reality.

Be

As we come to the end of the story, we are given a glimpse into the future. Now it is our task, as much as is possible in this age, to reveal the future in the present. As the Church, as well as individual Christians, we are to reveal what it looks like when God is in charge. Like actors on a stage, we are to demonstrate what it looks like when relationships are based on love and righteousness; where we are no longer slaves to sin and death, but are free to

182 WEEK 6

serve God with joy and power in the Holy Spirit; where we know and experience the love of God and allow it to flow out of our lives toward others around us; and where those things that divide us right now (race, class, gender, etc.) are not a source of division but are brought together in a beautiful unity that is full of diversity. The true nature of the kingdom of God should be seen in our marriages, our friendships, our families, and our churches. We are the people who declare that Jesus is Lord and that God raised Him from the dead. And we are the people who believe He is coming back to make all things new and to receive His own to Himself for all eternity!

Do

When we read the Scripture in the presence of the Holy Spirit and with the people of God, we find ourselves being changed. We become something that we were not before. Our thinking changes. Our attitude toward God and other people changes. Our understanding of who God is, what He is doing, and how we are involved is clarified.

Now that you are at the end of this journey, take a few moments to prayerfully think over the last few weeks. In what ways do you see yourself changing for the better

DAY 5: EDEN RESTORED 183

(in other words, becoming more like Jesus)? What things are you still struggling with? Write your thoughts here and then take them to the Lord in your prayer time. Thank Him for what He has already done in your life through these encounters, and commit to continue to encounter Him in this way as you continue your walk with Him. Be honest with Him about your struggles and allow Him to minister His grace and peace to you. Know that what God starts, He will finish. We have seen that from the biblical story.

> . . . being confident of this, that he who began a good work in you will carry it on to completion until the day of Christ Jesus (Philippians 1:6).

184 WEEK 6

Bibliography

Alexander, Ralph H. "Ezekiel." In *The Expositor's Bible Commentary: Jeremiah-Ezekiel*, edited by David E. Garland and Tremper Longman III. Grand Rapids, MI: Zondervan, 2010.

Augustine, Daniela C. *Pentecost, Hospitality, and Transfiguration: Toward a Spirit-Inspired Vision of Social Transformation.* Cleveland, TN: CPT Press, 2012.

Kaiser, Walter C. "Exodus." In *The Expositor's Bible Commentary: Genesis-Leviticus*, edited by David E. Garland and Tremper Longman III. Grand Rapids, MI: Zondervan, 2008.

LaSor, William Sanford, David Allan Hubbard, and Frederic William Bush. *Old Testament Survey: The Message, Form, and Background of the Old Testament.* 2nd ed. Grand Rapids, MI: Wm. B. Eerdman's Publishing Co., 1996. 1982.

Westminster Dictionary of Theological Terms. Louisville, KY: Westminster John Knox Press, 1996.

What Others Are Saying . . .

People of the Spirit: The Story of God and His People by J. Ben Wiles is a biblically and theologically sound discipleship study that is especially well suited for pastoral and congregational use. It amazingly manages the dual task of being both in depth and understandable. In other words, it is both theological and practical. Its narrative format makes its thorough presentations a pleasure to read. Readers may not realize that they are working through a rigorous systematic study of dynamic Christian truth because the style is so readily accessible and enjoyable. However, they will be no less challenged and stretched intellectually and spiritually. The clear and concise Leader's Guide helps empower pastors to lead their congregations into the doctrinal and spiritual formation so essential to authentic Christian discipleship. In a day when rampant relativism seems to rule a culture stubbornly inclined toward secularist and pluralist biases, and even Christians sometimes struggle with the challenges of relevant living as fully devoted disciples of Jesus Christ, this thoughtful study from a fervent Pentecostal perspective promises to be an excellent aid for believers desiring a closer walk with God marked by deep commitment and true consecration.

—Tony Richie, D.Min, Ph.D.
Adjunct Professor of Historical and Doctrinal Theology, Pentecostal Theological Seminary, Cleveland, TN; Lead Pastor New Harvest Church of God, Knoxville, TN

Ben Wiles has produced a wonderful tool for use in discipleship of the modern Christian. Coming from the heart of a pastor and scholar, this work will greatly aid any leader seeking to follow the command of Christ to make disciples. I highly recommend his means of discipleship!

—Toby S. Morgan
Arkansas Church of God Administrative Bishop